Special request:

When you have finished reading this book, pass it along to another man, possibly your son or son-in-law. Or you can donate it to your church library.

More copies can be ordered at $10.00 each online at http://meninbalance.org/book or by writing to

Men in Balance™
20908 N. Main Street
Cornelius, NC 28031
books@meninbalance.org

Printing and distribution of this book is made possible by a grant from ***Mark Mahoney,*** *a long-time supporter, to whom we offer sincere thanks!*

If you wish to make a donation by credit card or PayPal, go to http://meninbalance.org/donate now *or send a check to the address above.*

10lessonsformen.com

10 LESSONS FOR MEN

...AND HOW OUR PARTNERS CAN HELP

ISBN 978-0-692-92831-8

Edited by Jacob C. Ratliff

Men in Balance™ Press

10 Lessons for Men

...and How Our Partners Can Help

10lessonsformen.com

ACKNOWLEDGEMENTS

This book is dedicated to my wife, Emmie, my partner in life and business for nearly 30 years and without whose help and patience this book could never have happened.

Sincere thanks to the men referenced in this book who have openly shared and worked on issues important to them knowing they had the loving support of the others in the group.

As every writer knows, success is very dependent on many people who help you along the way. I'm especially grateful for the dedicated work done by writer/editor extraordinaire Jacob C. Ratliff in editing and proofing this manuscript numerous times. Also to long-time friend and writer, Jerry Blackwelder, for his excellent suggestions. Others I need to thank for their support and help:

Philip Loydpierson, MSW
Rev. Dr. John Rowe
Rev. Dr. Jody Seymour
Rev. Stephen Ratliff
Emmie Alexander Hancock
Jerry Blackwelder
Ed Boye
Chris Feigl
Paul Newton
Jack Jackson
Steve Iglehart
Roy Sinclair
Tom Rochester
Ted Schott
Jim Gilpin
Dennis Carrai
Jacob Ratliff
Kelly Williams
Suzanne Hurley
Mark Mahoney
Roger McCullough
Carmen DiGiandomenico
Cincinnati Men in Balance
Men in Balance™ donors

TABLE OF CONTENTS

WHO SHOULD READ THIS BOOK...

- **Men**
    - wishing to learn more about themselves and make changes to improve their marriages or intimate relationships
    - going through divorce or separation seeking to understand what went wrong
    - facing a "speed bump" in their life such as job loss, change of social status or health issues
    - looking for more substantive relationships with other men

- **Women**
    - who want to better understand their man and enrich their relationship

- who want to help their man become more fully human by learning about and accepting his masculine makeup
- hoping for more closeness in their relationships with men, including male family members.
- searching for relationships with men who can become loving husbands and fathers.

- **Mothers**
  - wanting for their sons a new paradigm of masculinity and what it can mean to be a man
  - wanting to understand their role in creating potential issues later in life for sons or daughters

- **Fathers**
  - wanting a closer relationship with sons and daughters
  - who may question their effectiveness as a parent of a son or stepson
  - wanting to lead their family spiritually

- **Counselors**
  - who may pass along some of these ideas to men seeking guidance
  - who wish to expand their understanding of

men's issues

- looking to develop more empathy for the issues men are facing

- **Ministers**
  - who are seeking a deeper understanding of men and how their church can help
  - planning to develop a new type of Men's Ministry more relevant to contemporary men (Men in Balance™ offers Men's Ministry programs based on these ideas. Page 203)

- **Sons**
  - who wish to have a better understanding of their father's heritage and belief system
  - working to understand the importance of the father/son relationship and its implication for their lives
  - hoping to someday father their own sons and daughters in more holistic ways

- **Daughters**
  - who want a better understanding of their fathers and the other men in their lives
  - who may feel their fathers parented them differently from their brothers

PURPOSE OF THIS BOOK….

This book is a collection of my own observations about men's issues based on 10 years of facilitating hundreds of small group and individual coaching sessions as well as serving as Executive Director of Men in Balance™, a non-denominational 501(c)(3) non-profit organization dedicated to the spiritual development of men.

The saddest realization for me in this work is that many men resist counseling or taking an introspective look at themselves, even when their job or marriage is threatened. It is my hope that in this book men may find answers to some of the troublesome questions they wrestle with daily about life, career, marriage, relationships, and spirituality.

"These women feel their men just don't get it."

INTRODUCTION

Statistics show more and more divorces are being initiated by wives instead of husbands. This is a new but growing trend. "Today Americans want not only a spouse who is reliable and reasonable, but also someone who is their best friend, and a great lover, and someone who pays the bills ... but is also really fun," said Stanford sociologist Michael Rosenfeld in an article in the *Washington Post*.[1]

According to research that Rosenfeld presented at the American Sociological Association's annual meeting, women's heightened expectations can leave them feeling worse off in marriage than men. In a survey of 2,262 adults in heterosexual partnerships over the course of five years, Rosenfeld found that 69% of divorces are initiated by women. On the whole, women also reported less satisfaction with their marriages than men. The reasons vary, but a common thread is wives being unhappy with their husbands' refusal to change.

As Executive Director of a non-profit called Men in Balance™, I have seen first-hand the wrecked relationships and damaged trust men are finding in their marriages and their lives. This is caused in many cases by hanging onto old ideas about manhood, marriage, and their role in a marriage or an intimate relationship. Counselors tell me that many times, wives have tried to drag husbands into therapy before eventually issuing an ultimatum: Change or the marriage is over.

These women feel their men "just don't get it." They can't understand why men won't allow themselves to be more fully human, to show heartfelt empathy, and, yes, vulnerability. They are no longer content to have someone who provides a good living and a comfortable lifestyle. They want connection--deep and soulful relating--and they believe they are entitled to it. It makes no sense to them that their man is singularly focused on career and accumulation of toys and trinkets at the expense of a rewarding family life and a true and equal partnership. (To be fair, there are a lot of men who DO get it, who have natures more compatible with what women are seeking. Some of them got that awareness after failing at one or more marriages.)

As for men, they may feel they are in an impossible Catch 22. They feel pressured to support an increasingly more costly standard of living (which they see as their main job description) but feel they are expected to do so without taking additional time from the family.

This book is about our relationships as men, the lessons we can learn, and how our partners can help us to become more human and relate more deeply. I believe you will find my observations and recommendations intriguing, whether you are the male or female in an intimate relationship. I hope to offer *practical, hands-on ideas and soul-searching questions* intended to bring about enduring improvements in relationships--and indeed, in the lives of men and their partners generally.

In a decade of working with men of all ages in small groups, dozens of personal coaching/counseling sessions, interviews, and years of coaching executives, I have learned there are lots of men who see themselves as clueless about relationships, especially intimate relationships. While they would "take a bullet" to protect their partner or loved one, they seem mystified about what else to do to maintain and grow the relationship--and equally in the dark about how or where to learn that.

How did this happen?
It's not all their fault. As men, we are conditioned (even rewarded) for placing minimal emphasis on relationships. But what's interesting is how women become unwitting accomplices--frequently giving us a free pass when we get it wrong, while at the same time demanding more substantive connection with us. A second Catch 22.

The cost to men for this "relationship clumsiness" is staggering, ranging from broken marriages and damaged children to derailed careers and unsuccessful business partnerships. I believe fixing this problem must be a joint enterprise between men and their partners.

This book is not just for men. If you are a woman, I hope you will use this book as an opportunity to empathically and lovingly nudge your man toward growth and personal development (vs. criticizing him). Each section ends with specific suggested actions for men *and* women.

Will Men Change?

While there are many men who are happy with their lives and for whom things are going well, there are many others who have real issues in their lives and don't know how to fix them. Here are some of the symptoms of unhappiness I hear mentioned often by men:

- Loss of zest for life--life is not turning out as he had envisioned it.
- Career disillusionment--realizing he likely will not be the CEO nor will he become a millionaire.
- A sense of isolation and spiritual emptiness, even though he may be attending worship services.
- In some cases, he may have become addicted to pornography, womanizing, alcohol, or drugs.
- Relationships are suffering. Because of the number of demands on his life, he has not paid attention to relationships and some are in poor repair.
- Work is crowding out most other things. While men pride themselves on their career, in many cases demands of work leave little room for other interests or personal growth.
- Demands of daily life can seem overwhelming and continuing to mount up. Feeling as though he is on a treadmill, he is chasing an ever-higher standard of

living for his family. But the cruel irony is that the work required to provide it takes him away from his family even more.

- His marriage is less satisfying, or he perceives that it is. He does not know how to fix it. And sex has become routine, boring, nonexistent, or illicit.
- There's a sense of fatalism. He doesn't see things getting better any time soon.

I have a lot of empathy for men and the pressures they feel. In session after session of our small group discussions, I feel I have heard it all.

Here are some of the main topics a man might bring up in these sessions:

- History of a bad relationship with his father
- Marriage difficulties that seem intractable, hard for him to understand
- Children who don't appreciate the standard of living being provided them
- A partner who doesn't understand the pressures he is feeling
- A wife who is critical instead of supportive of his efforts, especially in his career
- An inability to successfully manage conflict or a tendency to avoid conflict altogether
- Lack of close male friends with whom he can be open and honest

- A wife who asks him to be open but who cannot handle the honesty of his feelings, or so he feels
- A sense of not having the tools necessary to navigate the requirements of marriage and relationships

While some of these problems may seem to be of men's own making, they are nonetheless real. For example, a man may neglect relationships, then suddenly realize he has no close friends to confide in. Or he may avoid talking with his partner about how he truly feels, then wonder why she is not more sensitive to the pressures he is feeling.

There is some logic to how this happens, though it may be of little comfort to a man who has just hit a "speed bump" in his life, leaving him feeling very shaken up.

Here are some of the contributors to the suffering men feel:

- Men are typically not conditioned to nurture, so many of them do not maintain relationships well. They may feel relationship work "should not be so hard."
- Men are told by the culture that advancement in their career is supremely important, but if they focus too much on it, they get pushback at home.
- Many men identify with their career so totally that if they lose their job, they "lose" their identity, or so they think.

- Many men see themselves as less proficient in expressing themselves verbally, so they feel unable to hold their own with their partner in a sensitive or difficult conversation
- Because of their clumsiness or difficulty in expressing their feelings, many may feel they are not measuring up to their partner's expectations (and are told so)
- If they have unresolved issues with their fathers, they may feel insecure as men. But since it is not acceptable to show their insecurity, they mask it with false bravado or exterior toughness, alcohol, womanizing, or other bad habits.

Surprise! Men Want to Talk!
When I began working with men's groups, I was warned repeatedly that men will not talk in a group setting. They will not let themselves open up. They will not allow themselves to be vulnerable--especially with other men they may not know.

To my pleasant surprise, they DO want to talk! In all the sessions I have led, I have never experienced the uncomfortable silence of un-engaged men. Once they agree to confidentiality and learn other men are facing similar issues, they are all too ready to talk. It's as if they've been waiting for the right environment. And while the groups do not typically give advice, they do push each other to own up to their role in the difficulties they are facing.

Men do it differently

Some interesting things I have noticed about how men deal with each other that is different from women:

- Men seem to interrupt each other less often and don't finish each other's sentences as frequently. This may sometimes be unwillingness to confront.
- Men talk in shorthand. They may open with a cryptic statement, then elaborate, perhaps clumsily, as the words come to them. Additionally, they speak in slogan-like/cliché phrases using words sparsely.
- There's a heavy dose of logic in their talk, usually edging out much of the emotional content.
- Colorful detail and tangents are rare. Barebones narratives may be hard to follow, in fact. The details do come later as the picture unfolds.
- Emotions other than anger may be missing (men's anger is typically approved in our culture; other emotions less so).
- Men need a reason *why* something is happening--logic. The assumption is that once you know the reason something is happening, you can fix it. Men want results.
- Comments to others in a group can seem pretty "bare knuckles direct" at times, even brash. Respect may be there, but there may be little attempt to moderate the tone.
- They are reluctant to offer unsolicited advice,

referring to "other men they have known" as examples to learn from instead of saying, "Here's what I think you should do."

So what does all this mean?

1. Contrary to what wives/partners may feel, men *will* open up and share their frustrations and concerns. They do it differently to be sure. But if the environment is safe, they will talk.

2. Men are very concerned about their relationships and the communication that surrounds them, but may feel incapable of talking straightforwardly with women about their feelings.

3. The lack of success in having this kind of open conversation cripples close relationships and likely deprives men of connection with others (and themselves), producing an emotional and spiritual vacuum leading to more of the same.

My hope is that this book will

- help men find their spiritual bearings, openly dealing with issues in their own relationships
- offer hope for more robust and vibrant relationships with partners, families, and other men
- offer men a variation of the male model they may have embraced since childhood

Together, we will look at the societal factors which have contributed to the status quo. We will examine options to becoming "career addicts." We will dig deeper into the key ingredients which "make a man a man" or at least have traditionally defined men. And finally, we will attempt to re-map men's perception of themselves, allowing more acceptance of what it *can* mean to be a fully functioning man.

The 10 Lessons

The book is designed around 10 lessons which will help men be more fully human, more sensitive to the needs of their partners and other loved ones, and more willing to engage fully with these loved ones. It is also important to note the full title which includes the phrase ".....and how our partners can help," because women have a lot to gain from this book by working with and encouraging their man. I suggest you read this as a couple, discussing the concepts as you go, making this a mutual effort.

What else?

We will talk about important issues affecting men negatively including our own narrow view of masculinity, which constricts our engagement with others. We will explore our obsession with competition and independence and the accompanying costs to relationships. Of course, the costs of out-of-balance focus on career are covered as well.

As you might surmise, there is also a very real spiritual element to this, but you need not focus on your spiritual side to profit from this book. The ways spirituality might factor into the equation will be noted as we move along.

I welcome your feedback about the concepts in this book. You need not agree with my observations. My hope is that these ideas will stimulate further discussion in your marriage or close relationship as well as groups you participate in. Copies are available for group study.

I want to hear about your experiences. Contact me at jerry@meninbalance.org.

"Being the tough guy and always invulnerable simply does not work in the real world of work and relationships.

LESSON 1

BROADENING OUR NARROW VIEW OF MASCULINITY

Where did you get your ideas about what it means to be a man? Was it from your father? Was it from other men in the neighborhood, a teacher or coach, church, family members? Whatever the sources of our notions of manhood, they are from a select group or two, and as such, are inherently narrowly defined.

As men, why do we define ourselves so narrowly? If I ask you, as I did at a breakfast with about 60 attendees, to jot down 3 words that were used to define manhood when you were growing up, chances are you would write things like they did: strong, independent, great provider, never cries, individualistic, unemotional, "in charge."

If I ask you to write down some words to describe how you would like your son or grandson to see themselves, chances are you'd write words like empathic, sensitive, considerate, spiritual, tender-hearted.

Notice the disconnect? Isn't it interesting how the way society and our peers define manhood fails us? Being the tough guy, warrior, always “in charge,” and always invulnerable, simply does not work in the real world of work and personal relationships.

Many times, our independence and toughness cause us to be overly competitive, aggressive, and inappropriately defensive in relationships with colleagues--and especially so with our partners.

When I talk to women about what they want in a man, they talk about the qualities in the second list above. Being open, empathic, sensitive, responsive, tender-hearted and collaborative--these are the things that make for good relationships. Unfortunately, these are the things we weed out of young boys as they become men and instead encourage being individualistic, independent, tough and assertive.

Most often we get our view of masculinity from our father who likely got it from his father. Think about that. Your view of masculinity could be out-of-date by two generations! What is expected of you and me as a husband, father, or brother has changed dramatically in that time. Women are no longer content to be married to someone who can provide well for them--they expect deep emotional closeness, collaboration on decision making and some openness and willingness to be influenced on most issues—and rightfully so. (See **Introduction**). This willingness to be influenced may be the most valuable quality to strive for in your relationships and it is not just being a "nice guy." It is a new permanent way to operate because it reduces the need for her to "dig in her heels" on a position.

A significant problem in many marriages is that of a man seeing his role only as the breadwinner with little other responsibility or interaction in the family. It may not seem fair to realize that the long hours we put in at work and the impressive job we do providing for the family is seen as not nearly enough. And yet many of us were taught that if a man provided well for his family, he was fulfilling the marital contract quite successfully.

According to Terrence Real in *The New Rules of Marriage*, that model of masculinity went away decades ago, and yet many men continue to operate as though it still works. He also notes that women's roles have changed even more than men's roles have, which causes confusion.[1] It seems many men think of marriage as though it were an appliance--you plug in it and it should be good to go for about 20 years.

Maybe you have received feedback from your partner about the way you relate to her or the family. You may also have received feedback about how open you are (or are not) in conversation with your partner. These should be red flags for you to investigate and make changes accordingly, especially if you are using a communication model similar to Dad's.

A really good reason for you to change is the likelihood that your sons are observing the model of masculinity you project and are subconsciously making a decision about what it means to be a man, and how a man is supposed to treat women. That alone is reason for you to investigate how you might revise your view of masculinity. (See the lesson on **Our Attitude Toward Women**.)

Expressing Emotion

Our narrow view of masculinity also may inhibit us from expressing emotion where it is clearly needed. I can think of a time when I was in the presence of a young boy on a group camping trip when he received news that his father had died. For whatever reason, I simply sat there as a spectator when I should have immediately gone to him, embraced him and reassured him as best I could. Inexplicably, I was silent and unemotional, maybe unsure what to do, like all the other men present. I think many men can identify with that experience. Expression of empathy is probably the least used and yet possibly the most important emotion we can summon in many circumstances. Most women do this automatically, but we tend to freeze up when it is required of us.

It is sad that we even sometimes have trouble with grief--even natural grief that follows the loss of a job or going through divorce. We have not been taught how to experience or express grief other than at funerals. However, my experience is that men are typically very grief-stricken by divorce or even a casual relationship breakup. We cover it well or at least try to because we believe that's what is expected.

It's not that we cannot display emotion -- just look at how we behave when we are angry. We've said society gives us permission as men to be angry, but we don't believe it gives us permission to express other emotions, especially tender emotions. For example, I have heard from many men who are not able to enjoy play activities with their children, and their reason is they feel it makes them look less masculine. What could be more masculine than participating in child play with your own offspring? If you're that concerned about your male image in this most important yet tender activity, there's a good chance both you and your children will one day be regretting those missed opportunities.

What do women want?

Based on the research, women are clearly expecting more emotional connection in relationships. This may make us feel "pressured" to be expressive when we are not feeling like being expressive, or feel we don't know how. It may seem that women are putting extreme pressure on us to accommodate them emotionally. Actually, they have every right to expect us to be fully present and emotionally interactive with them and the family. Yet this concern about potentially appearing vulnerable, especially with our partner, keeps us at a distance and makes true intimacy impossible. In other words, we maintain our distance emotionally to protect our ego and our (outdated) view of masculinity even though it eventually weakens or destroys our relationship with the one(s) we love. Where is the logic in that?

If this pressure to be more open with our loved ones causes us to feel emasculated or less than our masculine selves, it is probably time to do some soul-searching. Think about it. What is lost by being emotionally expressive with your wife and children? By contrast, what is the *payoff* of this behavior? It's not as though someone is making impossible demands of us. It is just that we have been taught to keep our emotions at bay and never give *anyone* ammunition they might use to hurt us later. This approach may have been helpful in prehistoric times since you were in constant competition with every other male to provide food for your family. But it doesn't make sense to hang on to that idea in the 21st century, does it?

Here's something else we lose with our narrow view of masculinity: We give up our interest in things that may appear feminine such as art, music, or cooking when, actually, we might excel at and enjoy those activities. How often have you heard of men who, late in their lives, decide to become chefs or musicians or artists working with flowers? By this time the spiritual urge to be more complete insists on being heard, and the result is a more whole and fulfilled individual. "Men need to understand they can be nurses or hairdressers without losing their masculinity."[2] The so-called mid-life crisis is also a sign of a "spiritual anemia," a longing for something with real meaning. More on this in **Lesson 6** ***Why Our Focus on Career Robs Us of Connection***.

Being "right"

I'm not sure how this became a masculine trait, but it appears to be: the emphasis on being "right." Many men are willing to go to the mat to prove they are right, and some have paid for it with their lives. Think about what happens if we carry this idea too far in our marriages or close relationships. Suddenly, we're seen as insensitive men who must have their way at the expense of others or whose ego is too weak to admit a mistake. Either comparison is unflattering, to say the least. The need to be right, by the way, is closely tied to the unwillingness to forgive. When we refuse to forgive, it is as though we have decided to carry around indefinitely this huge weight the other person has likely already forgotten about. But our insistence that we have been wronged allows us to stubbornly persist in consuming a lot of energy and time for no good reason. As noted elsewhere, forgiveness is not something we do for the other person. It is something we do for ourselves.

Male Friends

Years ago, I was with a group of men chatting informally over coffee. The movie *Brokeback Mountain* had recently been released. One brave man brought it up for discussion mentioning the close relationship between the two main characters. It soon became clear that the other men did not want to talk about the movie. He persisted. "If you took the sex out of it, could you see yourself having a lifelong close relationship like that with another man?" he asked. No takers. The other men were too uncomfortable to even entertain the question. Sad.

I was with another group when one older man, who had recently become somewhat disabled, volunteered that he had to call in an electrician to change a bulb in a fixture on a high ceiling. "I had to leave the room while he did it," he said. "As a man, I just couldn't stand not being able to fix it myself." His identity as a man was very rigid and he was embarrassed to be unable to do "manly" things. Since I know his family, I am certain that his daughters and wife never considered this incident to be related to his masculinity.

What do YOU want?

I think what men want most for themselves is to be authentic men. Not the image society places on them, not the roles family or job gives them, but free to be who they are—men in the truest sense. No need to clean up your act, be more politically correct, conform to someone's idea of what a man is. The cruel irony here is that the path to being more authentic involves just the kind of things we are discussing in this book. The first step on this path is to reject the stereotype we have been prisoner to, and, in concert with a loving partner, redefine ourselves more holistically and less narrowly. That is why a conversation with your partner is both essential and liberating.

Following are some suggestions as well as hard questions to ask yourself about your view of masculinity and whether it deserves another look. My suggestion is that you allow yourself to be vulnerable enough to think honestly about this issue and what price you may be paying by hanging onto an outdated concept. If you really want to know the truth about how you are perceived, be brave enough to ask your wife or partner. Let her know you want brutal honesty in her answer and likely she will give it to you. Just remember not to defend your behavior or make excuses. All you can say to the feedback is "Thank you."

Summary

It is likely we copied the model of masculinity we saw in our fathers and other men in our early lives. It is also likely that model is no longer working for us. Today, women are expecting a lot more from us and that includes genuine closeness, expression of our emotions, and true connection. Whether we admit to needing that connection as well, our lives are much richer when we allow ourselves to be open and vulnerable with the persons we love. A conversation with our partner is a good starting point to assure her that we understand how important this is to her and begin to learn how we might change to better meet her needs.

The Balanced Approach

There is plenty of room to strike a balance between a tough guy, macho, warrior style and one of openness and willingness to be genuine with your loved ones.

Keeping your balance

On the scale below put a ^ mark where you think you are in your view of masculinity and another ^ where you would like to be and will work toward.

|---|

I could use some improvement in my view of masculinity	I have a very healthy view of masculinity

Soul-Searching Questions

- Are you willing to have another look at your ideas about masculinity? Are you willing to enlist your partner in discussing this?
- Does the idea of pursuing interests such as cooking or painting or writing seem less than masculine to you?
- Are you willing to quietly work on allowing your "softer, gentler side" to show, at least at home with an openness that may allow vulnerability?
- Does the fact that there are great male artists, writers, poets and chefs influence your thinking about what is masculine?
- If you have sons, are you comfortable with them adopting your model of masculinity? If you have daughters, are you comfortable with their future husbands adopting your model?
- Have you ever felt you were "missing out" in some emotional events, such as a sad movie or a funeral, because you could not let your emotions show?
- Where are some small ways you can begin to be more demonstrable emotionally as you try on new behaviors?
- Objectively, what are the reasons for/against making a change?

Action Steps Men Can Take

- Check out some books about masculinity. (See the **Resources** section or visit the Men in Balance™ website.)
- Talk to your son about how he sees masculinity and listen for how he sees you in this regard.
- Bring up this topic in a discussion with another man. Compare views. Be open, non-defensive.
- Ask your partner for thoughts about this topic (not whether you measure up to some standard). Prepare to be surprised.
- Google the topic "masculinity in different cultures."
- Talk openly to your minister or a counselor.
- If you are really brave, seek out a gay man to talk with. Gay men, out of necessity, tend to be more plugged into their emotional side.
- Record your commitments on the Personal Action Plan on page 194.

Action Steps Women Can Take

- Initiate a discussion with your partner about masculinity. Share your ideas about the topic. Talk about behaviors, not abstract concepts. Be patient with his struggles in this area.
- Get a book on this topic and read it with your partner, pausing frequently for discussion.
- Be firm, but empathic, with your man if you believe there is more to masculinity than macho behavior.
- Above all, assure your partner that his feelings about this topic are safe and confidential with you. NEVER violate that.
- Be on the lookout for movie or TV characters displaying a non-traditional view of masculinity. Discuss with your man.
- Check out your children's views on this, especially teens. Probe for details. Compare their ideas to your own views.
- If your partner already demonstrates a good model in this area, tell him directly.

"What's really at work when we resist opening up is the sense of vulnerability it produces."

Lesson 2
Improving Our Attitudes Toward Women

What's that you say? You say you don't have a problem with your attitude toward women? Heaven knows we all love them, but it is hard to acknowledge that we likely have an outdated view of women. In some ways, we may still actually regard them as inferior. Of course, none of us would ever admit that openly, but it's true that many of us have received feedback from our women about how we treat them, even unintentionally.

Much like our notions of masculinity and manhood, a lot of our views about women are likely "inherited" from our fathers' view, since most of us adopted many of our fathers' beliefs without question. Unless you were lucky enough to have a father with a healthy view of women, it's likely you inherited a few unconscious biases as well.

The Problem

The problem simply stated is that our unexamined views of women sometimes cause us to disregard their input, resist or fail to share power with them, and fail to learn from their often superior emotional intelligence.

Let's unpack that statement. In household matters, it's impossible to disregard a woman's input as she may speak very directly about how she wants things to be. On such matters, women feel a certain empowerment to speak up because this tends to be an area of huge importance for them and one in which they are traditionally viewed as the experts. On other matters, however, such as how to spend discretionary money, she may yield to your preferences just to keep the peace and avoid confrontation. That doesn't mean she agrees or has no opinion, but if she has been conditioned to be less assertive, she may fail to speak up.

As for sharing power with women, what else could they want? Their name is on the bank accounts and the deed. They often decide where to go on vacation, which church to attend, and a host of other family decisions. But true power-sharing, especially as a woman might see it, involves collaboration and thinking through options together in an open atmosphere where both parties feel comfortable expressing themselves. Feeling heard.

As men, we tend to speak boldly and forcefully and to put our ideas on the table pretty quickly. But if we do not show some patience and willingness to be influenced by our partner's opinion, we can come off as rigid and arbitrary—even rude. To your partner, it may seem the decision is already made, or that it would be futile to challenge it.

How many times has it happened to you that you have stated your point of view to your partner only to find out later that she had a different perspective but didn't speak up at the moment because it seemed your mind was made up. This is often a source of frustration for men: We expect people who have a different point of view to voice it. But, for a woman, that may be difficult because she doesn't have a lot of history of that working for her. In other words, she may be expecting "softer" statements *("I'm considering" vs. "I'm going to...")* which allow for another point of view or the invitation to influence decisions. And she may see your assertive "action statement" as final and not to be questioned. Women are often conditioned to give up their boundaries for the sake of peace and harmony. But that doesn't mean the issue is closed. I've heard men say that women not being honest about what they are feeling is often the cause of a fight. Generally, it sounds like men should speak a little less forcefully and women a little more so.

What we can do, of course, is state frequently that we are open to hearing other ideas from her, but that statement needs to be accompanied by some actions that support it. If we have positions of power at work (if we are the person "in charge") we may be even more likely to forget the importance of real collaboration--although sometimes job performance feedback may remind us.

As for a woman's superior emotional intelligence, most men likely would not challenge that assumption. As men, we are not encouraged to learn the subtler points of relationships and interpersonal negotiation. As a consequence, we can appear brusque and even harsh in interactions with our partners.

We need to talk...

This is the phrase that puts fear in the hearts of men when our partner says this to surface an issue. We'll talk more about communication issues later, but for now let's talk about the vulnerability we feel when our partners ask us to speak openly with them. One of the most common complaints I hear is:

"My wife expects me to 'open up and share' but I'm not sure she can handle what's really on my mind and therefore I bite my tongue in order to protect her."

That's likely not a good idea because it is based on *your* understanding of her capacity to handle something, and it denies her the chance to speak for herself. It's smarter to assume that she *can* handle what's on your mind and that she *wants* to hear it. The simple fact that you are trying to protect her might mean you need to investigate your attitudes about women, especially your partner.

Vulnerability

What's really at work when we resist opening up is the sense of vulnerability it produces. In fact, the word vulnerability is typically missing from our vocabulary because, as men, we see it as a weakness. Talk about contrast! For your partner, vulnerability simply means openness and honesty--and those are signs of strength, not weakness. But to avoid showing any weakness, we often keep our deepest fears and concerns to ourselves. We rationalize that we are "taking care of her" as we have been taught to do. Reminder: She likely has not asked for protection. My former pastor, Dr. Jody Seymour, talks of "appropriate vulnerability" which is not emotional nakedness, but a willingness to do some self-disclosure, especially about feelings.

The problem of withholding our feelings from our partners is that it denies us true intimacy with the person from whom we most need openness, trust and closeness. As a result, we feel isolated and deprived of a closeness to which we feel entitled as a partner. But we place the blame on her, not ourselves. This almost always breeds growing resentment as the behavior continues. And our women may feel we are emotionally distant, aren't willing to share, don't view them as equals, or just don't care.

Incidentally, the root of the word vulnerability is from the Latin "vulneris" or wound. So the question we face is whether we are willing to let our partner see our (emotional) "wound" or whether we will keep it covered in hopes neither she nor anyone else will hurt us further. The cruel paradox here is that we try not to appear vulnerable as a way of controlling events and keeping ourselves from experiencing pain. But in truth, realizing we never *really* have control over people or events can bring a real strength and peace of mind. Personally, that took me some time to digest.

Chores

Another example of not accepting true equality in the relationship is when we shift our share of the housework to our partner even if she is the primary breadwinner or working equivalent hours.

How much do you help out around the house, especially in the kitchen? Or how often do you do a load of clothes, including folding and putting them away? Shopping? Cooking? Getting kids to bed?

I talked to a man recently who told me he firmly believes that providing a good income for the family and the benefits of a good lifestyle should be enough. He doesn't feel he should have to do "housework." It happens that his wife also has a full-time job and there are three kids to be tended to daily. He says he doesn't mind dropping them off at school, but beyond that, he feels household duties should be a woman's job.

If this sounds like you, I hope you will examine your feelings. In today's environment with both parents working, there are more chores at home than one person can do. Besides, helping out as much as you can will free up time for your wife to spend with you! Not cheerfully helping can create resentment and a sense of unfairness on her part which can kill closeness.

There can also be some good communion time doing chores together. As one slogan said, "No man was ever stabbed to death doing the dishes."

Sex Objects

In his book *Straight Talk for Men About Marriage,* Martin G. Friedman discusses what men view to be the purpose of marriage. His findings show that "sex" is near the top of the list, suggesting that many men consider sex to be a primary purpose of marriage.[1]

Many of us have developed a confused notion about women and sex. Our earliest exposure to the titillation of sexual excitement can cause us to see only the physical attributes of a woman (which are plenty exciting), and fail to think about her deeper, more substantive qualities. So we unconsciously begin thinking of women in terms of what they can provide for us sexually. Indeed, men are conditioned from birth to objectify women and to view them as one-dimensional beings.[2] When we combine that with our clumsiness in conversation, it can leave a woman feeling that we are only interested in her ability to satisfy us sexually. As you may have experienced, this is deadly for a relationship with a woman and can make her feel devalued and disrespected. It would make you feel that way too. Her feelings may come as a surprise to us when we are trying so desperately to protect her and take care of her. But the combination of our behaviors may send a very different message.

Pornography

Pornography is so ubiquitous in today's society that it is almost dismissed as routine and benign. Dismissing its potential for damage is a real mistake in terms of our relationships with the women we love. In his book *How Can I Get Through to You: Closing the Intimacy Gap Between Men and Women,* Terrence Real writes, "Even when not overtly aggressive, pornography posits women as existing for men's use."[3] (See **Resources.**) Porn supposedly gives men a sense of power and prestige in that these women are available to *him* (which completely ignores the fact they are available to anybody). But there is plenty of documentation showing that involving ourselves in pornography leads us to think of women as sex objects, which makes it nearly impossible to think of them as equal partners in a loving relationship. According to *everydayhealth.com* It also can lead to erectile dysfunction, even in young men.

Our Daughters

Our view of women can cause subtle differences in the way we relate to our daughters as opposed to our sons.

With our sons, we typically encourage action-oriented independence and confident decision-making. Treating our daughters differently can sometimes create a distance between us and them. But more importantly, it can damage their self-confidence and self-esteem. If they don't believe that we think of them as competent and capable, it's hard for them to think of themselves that way. This is a unique gift that men can give their daughters. If we are overprotective of our daughters, we teach them to be helpless and not to trust their own judgment or ability. Just like our sons, they need to receive our blessing, typically defined as a distinct, pro-active message in which we acknowledge them as a fully functioning, capable, independent person. This assures them they are capable of making their own way in a challenging world. We should also acknowledge that our wives and daughters don't always need our protection.[4]

Women at Work

If we are not aware of how our attitude toward women is failing to serve us, we may inadvertently treat the women we work with in a less than appropriate way. If we fail to show proper respect for them and value their input in teams or other collaborative efforts, we send the message that we are clinging to yesterday's view of women –– and that will likely come back to haunt us.

Research shows that men interrupt women more than they do other men—and more than women interrupt others.[5] The result is that we lose the benefit of women's thinking and experience. If a woman speaks up, the men often ignore her input and talk to each other.

I have talked with a number of men who report to female managers on the job who have issues arising from their own prejudices--or their boss *perceiving* that they have prejudices. Further, the more we see women mainly as sex objects, the more likely we are to engage in inappropriate relationships in the workplace such as affairs or sexual harassment. This can result in our losing our job or damaging key relationships at a minimum. In many cases there are actual punitive consequences for such behavior. We have certainly seen a large number of prominent men torpedo their careers with just this sort of behavior.

Just a note to conclude: If your view of women is that they are primarily to be protected and sheltered, you might ask first if she wants that. Some do, but some might find it offensive. Still, I would say opening the car door for her is better than just using the remote. Helping her with her chair at a restaurant is still a good thing. Chivalry is not totally dead. If you are unclear about her preferences, ask her.

Summary

Most of us could use some work in our attitudes toward women. Through our conditioning, we have learned bad habits that have harmed us in our connection with our partners, our daughters and sometimes our female co-workers or managers. While we may *appear* to have less emotional intelligence than some women, we can improve our communication and our relationships with women by using more collaborative and egalitarian approaches. The payoff for this is a level of intimacy, partnership, and connectedness with our women that we may never have experienced.

Stonewalling and pretending that we have no issues in this area does not help us get to where we need to be.

The Balanced Approach

We must recognize the equality of women in all we do while, at the same time, ask about her preferences if we are uncertain.

KEEPING YOUR BALANCE

On the scale below put a ^ mark where you think you are in your attitude toward women and another ^ where you would like to be and will work toward.

|---|

I could use some improvement in my attitude toward women	I have a very healthy attitude toward women

Soul-Searching Questions

- In what areas of your life have you been guilty of a poor attitude toward women? How is this affecting your relationships with your partner, your daughters, your sisters, and work associates?
- What was your father's view of the way to treat women? Do you subscribe to that view? What changes would you make?
- Do you have a daughter? Would you be comfortable if she married someone with your view of women? How would that help/harm her?
- Do you have sons? Are you treating them differently than you would a daughter? How so? Why?
- Have you found yourself passing along jokes or emails which stereotype or disrespect women ("all in good fun")?
- After reading this chapter, what changes do you want to make in your own life?
- Do you agree that, as men, our attitude toward women can cause problems in relationships? Why or why not?
- Are you involved in pornography? How do you think that involvement is impacting your view of women or your relationship with your partner?
- Are you involved in an affair, justifying it because of problems at home?

Action Steps Men Can Take

- Initiate a discussion with your wife asking for feedback about how you interact with her, what she needs more of, less of.

- Pay attention to your language. Do you find yourself referring to adult women, especially in the office, as "girls" or even more derogatory terms? If so, drop that language immediately.

- Are you pulling your weight on household duties? Empty the dishwasher, vacuum the floor, clean up the kitchen, do the laundry frequently.

- Collaborate with your wife to make consensus decisions (e.g. purchases, choice of restaurant, financial decisions).

- End any use of pornography. Examine why you are drawn to it. Get counseling if needed before it causes problems in your relationships.

- Increasingly share your fears and concerns with your partner to assure yourself she cares and can handle them. I almost guarantee she can.

- If you are in an affair, get some counseling for yourself and find a way to end it before it wrecks your life.

Action Steps Women Can Take

- Gently, lovingly, firmly, correct your man when he says things that are sexist or derogatory about women.
- Initiate a discussion with him about this topic to learn how he came to his views. Stay on topic. Make "I" Statements, not "You" statements. (For example, "I feel better when you..." vs. "You always do...")
- Monitor yourself to make sure you aren't encouraging negative views of women such as laughing at sexist jokes, for example.
- Reassure your partner that it is safe to talk about this or any other topic with you.
- Ask for what you want and need. Don't expect him to read your mind.
- Help him to learn how to show he loves and respects you (reward the good behaviors).
- Make your preferences clear about such things as helping you with your chair, opening the car door, etc.
- If your partner already demonstrates a good model in this area, tell him directly.

Notes from this section....

"If you feel you cannot truly be yourself with your partner and express your fears and worries as well as your happiness and success, something is missing."

LESSON 3

REMOVING OUR FEAR OF REAL INTIMACY (OR CONFUSION ABOUT SEX AND INTIMACY)

Intimacy Redefined

If you want some really interesting conversation, compare notes with your wife or partner about the meaning of intimacy. If you are hoping she will connect it to sex, you may be disappointed. For a woman, intimacy more often means safety, the assurance that she can be totally open and vulnerable with you and that you will not exploit that. That she can tell you her deepest fears and concerns and you will not use that against her later in a fight or some other conversation. Good definition, I'd say.

If that comes as a surprise to you, I suggest you look at your own ideas about intimacy and where you got those ideas. It is hard to be truly intimate with another person and maintain a warrior--macho, "tough guy" exterior. If you feel you cannot truly be yourself with your partner and express your fears and worries as well as your happiness and success, something is missing.

In his short, but powerful book *Love is Letting Go of Fear*, Gerald Jampolsky says all our behavior is driven by either love or fear. Sometimes we refuse to love completely because of our own fear of rejection or hurt. Learning to operate totally out of love (and trust) takes a special kind of dedication but it is worth it.

You Can Change This

In an interview on Men in Balance Radio, Davidson Basketball Coach Bob McKillop says the way we show our care for others is how much we give them these things: Time and Love. How much time do you spend with your partner in real closeness, excluding sexual contact? Do you, for example, spend a few minutes each night or at mealtime decompressing with each other before you go to bed, sharing your day and talking about what is on your mind? Are you comfortable bringing up concerns or worries you may have about personal things? Are you truly willing to listen and engage with her about her feelings about the relationship or other things that may be troubling her?

In our survey, 66% of men said they would like more conversation with their wife, but 42% said they did not know how to have a productive conversation with their partner on sensitive issues. Interestingly, 56% said they would like to be able to open up more with their wife.[1]

What is in there?

I am troubled by the number of men who are so out of touch with their own feelings that when I ask them how they feel about something, they say they don't know. It's as if they looked inside and found nothing there to report. They are what some women label as “locked up.” This is not acceptable. We have feelings and we must make the effort to reach inside ourselves, identify what we are feeling and share that with our loved ones, especially our partner. A teacup at a time if necessary at first, we must dip from that ocean inside us and pour it on the ones we love.

Whatever you may have been thinking about intimacy, this is where it really happens: in being able to be open and vulnerable with your partner and sharing your thoughts, including those that are not very "manly.” This should be the time when you can be emotionally honest with the person who knows you best and is most committed to your success. A time when you can be fully human and fully present in a love relationship, even creating a time of mutual spiritual renewal. And don’t be afraid of your feelings. Feelings are, by definition, fleeting and emotional and can change rapidly.

Does this idea of increasing your openness with your wife seem intriguing to you? Not every man can admit that he needs this kind of time with his partner but I'm convinced that most every man longs for it. If this kind of time is not happening in your marriage, ask yourself why not? If this is something you want, why is it not happening? If you believe the reason it is not happening is that your partner is not capable or not willing, you might reconsider that. Put the request on the table *("Honey, I need more quality time with you, more time just talking and enjoying each other's company. Would you be willing to help me make that happen? Here’s what I would like...")*

If you feel you have tried this before with no success, I beg you to try again after re-reading this chapter. You will need to start with a clean slate, forgiving any past transgressions of your partner.

If the issue is that you have hang-ups about allowing yourself to be this vulnerable, you are missing some real soul-satisfying moments because of a questionable, maybe even dangerous, belief. Additionally, what do you see as the purpose of marriage if it is not all defenses-down deep communion with each other? Too often we convince ourselves that our partner is not interested in or willing to meet our needs, so we don't ask. Or we miss the message she is trying to send that she can't feel really close to us when our behavior is insensitive, critical, judgmental or looking to place blame. If you are an "empty nester," you may have gotten out of the habit of simply enjoying each other because of the stresses of raising kids. You can have that again!

What's Your Problem?

A disturbing tendency I have noticed in men in some of my sessions is this temptation for a man to blame his partner for the lack of intimacy in their marriage. He sometimes describes his wife as cold, insensitive or unresponsive to his overtures. It's as if she is just being difficult or arbitrary or stingy with her affection. Sometimes he considers or has an affair out of spite, feeling his partner's behavior justifies it.

Rationally, men know an affair is not a solution and it is fraught with minefields for the marriage, but there is this pent-up anger to get back at his wife for his *perception* of the way she is treating him. The emphasis becomes totally based around the physical intimacy he needs and little on the emotional and psychological intimacy she may be needing. We may show our anger at the situation but we are not offering a solution or indicating our willingness to pursue one. (Interestingly, according to goodtherapy.com, anger issues are the main reason men end up going to counseling.[2]

This is immature behavior. If you find yourself in this situation or something similar, here is a checklist to ensure you are "keeping your side of the street clean" before you hurl accusations.

I feel the need to put in a disclaimer. All my suggestions in this book are assuming you are in a relationship with a rational, emotionally mature person, someone who is working honestly to keep the marriage healthy and satisfying. Someone willing to get counseling for her problems if that is required and willing to join you in counseling about the relationship, and someone who is willing to own her own issues. If that is not what you are dealing with, then a different approach is called for. *See page 203 for options.*

Now the checklist:

1) Talk to her honestly and openly, speaking about your emotional needs honestly and unapologetically. *"Honey, what I need from you is...."*

2) Make a straightforward and very specific request about your needs. Focus on behaviors you wish to see or not see. *"I would really appreciate it if you would greet me with a kiss when I come home."* This is different from a complaint *"You always" or "You never" do ......"*

3) Ask for her reaction to your needs. Listen without interruption or challenge or defensiveness. *"I really want to hear how you feel about this."*

4) Paraphrase back accurately what you hear. *"So it sounds like you are saying...."*

5) Keep doing this until she confirms you understand her point of view. Don't challenge or bring up other issues! These are her feelings and they are legitimate, not to be argued with.

6) Ask her to engage in a discussion about next steps such as trying some new approaches, getting counseling, hammering out an agreement. *"What would you like to see as our next steps toward resolving this?"*

7) Regardless of what she says, thank her for hearing your concerns. Be careful not to follow that with a complaint. *"I genuinely appreciate you opening up and sharing this with me. I want to take some time to think about what I heard. Then I will be able to give you a more thoughtful response."*

8) Spend some time thinking about what she said and what *you* have been contributing to the problem. If you can, acknowledge you have been guilty of some bad behavior. Apologize for that and make a focused effort to change. *"I need to admit that I have done X or Y and that has not been helpful for us. I apologize for that and I hope you will forgive me. I am committed to doing better."*

There is no guarantee that you will be satisfied with the outcome of this discussion. Remember, you don't have to resolve issues instantly. Such efforts may take several conversations and perhaps some counseling, but your focus should be on developing a *process* to resolve differences. That, in my opinion, is what successful couples have learned.

By the way, it is encouraging to hear that, according to Dr. John Gottman in *The Seven Principles for Making Marriage Work,* you can have a good marriage without ever resolving major differences. In fact, most major differences will never be resolved. And your marriage can survive even times of shouting at each other in an argument.[3] Feel better?

Also, Pat Love says in her book, *How to Improve Your Marriage Without Talking About It*, that you can make real improvements in your marriage without involving your partner. This means just working on your own issues quietly and alone. It's not a guarantee to keep you out of the counselor's office, but it's a good place to start.

Viagra Doesn't Create Intimacy

There is research to show that increasingly younger and younger men are depending on erectile dysfunction drugs in their marriage or intimate relationships. The research also shows that after a while, these drugs do not solve the problem because the unresolved issues in the relationship are more potent than the drugs (forgive the pun). Our focus on solving a sexual problem ignores the main culprit--our own brain. The body may be wanting physical closeness, but the emotional part of our brain is saying, "Not so fast. I've got some issues here!" Sadly, only about half the men in our survey (51%) report having a satisfying sex life at home and over 25% say they have lost enthusiasm for the relationship; 63% say they want more sex than they are getting.[4]

If unresolved issues are keeping you from feeling at peace with your partner, the hydraulics are simply not going to work. Therefore, finding a way to increase emotional, not physical, closeness is the only option. I'm sympathetic to men about this because most of us have never been taught how to put our guard down and be truly close to our partner. We are sometimes able to compartmentalize sex in a way that separates it from real intimacy, but eventually the soul wants more--it wants integration of our whole self in this most important part of ourselves.

For the future

For those of us who have had to start this journey of leaving behind our outdated views of what we consider manly in terms of emotional expression and intimacy, we know this is not easy. But the rewards are plentiful. Imagine being truly yourself, *emotionally transparent* with your partner and feeling relaxed instead of stressed about it. Imagine getting rid of any need for defensiveness or protectiveness when you are with the one you love. Imagine feeling the stirrings of an erection just thinking about this person and sensing that she feels equally aroused by thoughts of you. This type of intimacy is certainly worth pursuing, and if your own beliefs or conditioning are making it difficult or impossible to achieve this, it is probably time for some reflection or even counseling. Your partner will thank you for your effort and you will be closer to understanding what true "manliness" can be.

10 Reasons Guys Don't Get More Sex (in no particular order)

I included this section just because it is so interesting. In one of our sessions, we brainstormed why men aren't getting the sex they claim they want. Here's what we came up with:

- Whining about it/the lack of it (vs. talking about our needs)

- Playing it "cool" to see if she will initiate it (vs. initiating it lovingly without worry about rejection). Avoiding rejection is a sure way to avoid getting what you want.

- Acting angry or hurt, hoping for her to "make it right" (vs. making a request or being loving and cheerful). In one of our sessions, a man said, "My wife should know when I need sex—I'm irritable and unhappy." I responded, "So when she sees you are irritable and mad at her, that should be her cue

to initiate sex?" He wasn't happy with my challenge, but a lot of us have likely tried this approach.

- Not asking directly for what we want (vs. speaking up for ourselves)
- Complaining about what she has done/not done lately (vs. requesting something different)
- Waiting till bedtime to initiate affection (vs. demonstrating affection throughout the day)
- Answering in one-word answers or grunts and groans (vs. engaging in meaningful conversation with her)
- Making sex into a "project" to be completed perfectly (vs. allowing it to unfold based on each other's appetite)
- Skipping the relaxed conversation, the "I love you" kind of chat (vs. taking the time to learn about *her* and *her* feelings)
- Hint: Demonstrating your feelings of rejection is not a strategy nor is "wishing and hoping." Put the ego away and enjoy her!

BIG question: Are you brave enough to talk about this list with your partner?

Summary

As men, sometimes we get confused about intimacy and sex. If we think more deeply, we can understand that intimacy is a special kind of closeness that we need as much as our partner. It involves an emotional trust that goes far deeper than sex and begins with true friendship. To have true intimacy with our partner, we need to better understand her and listen attentively to her concerns, provide her safety in the relationship and make her feel cherished. When there's an issue we must own up to the part of the problem we created. The rewards for this are a closeness we long for but may never have experienced.

The Balanced Approach

Keep your passion for your partner alive, speak up for your needs lovingly and make her feel safe in the relationship. Remember we more often fail to meet each other's needs out of forgetfulness, not maliciousness.

Soul-Searching Questions

- Are you guilty of blaming your partner for your needs not being met?
- Are you willing to re-consider your ideas about sex, intimacy and manliness?
- Are you willing to commit to making some personal changes in order to truly experience intimacy?
- Are you doing everything you can to let your partner know how special she is to you *outside the bedroom*?
- Are you asking for what you need versus acting hurt?
- Are you making yourself available for simple conversation and listening time?
- Is the intimacy model you have one you would want for your children?
- Can you think of some loving ways to initiate sexual closeness without coming on like an animal?

Action Steps Men Can Take

- Initiate conversations with your partner about what intimacy means to each of you.
- Resolve to openly and unapologetically ask for what you need. Learn to deal with your fear of rejection.
- Get some counseling or do further reading on the topic of masculinity and intimacy.
- Abolish any thoughts of infidelity. Focus all your emotional energy lovingly on your partner.
- Stop blaming and start trying to understand and forgive.
- Renew your vows.
- Watch some romantic movies together and talk about them honestly.
- NEVER say, "I'm just not the mushy type. I am who I am."
- Don't harbor grudges. Get issues on the table or dismiss them.
- Look for signs of willingness to reconcile when there is conflict and hints of a need for closeness as well.
- Remember commitment to the relationship is a decision you make fresh every day and it is the same for her.
- Don't label the situation as hopeless or a standoff when there is conflict. Hang in there and keep showing acts of love.
- Record your commitments on the Personal Action Plan on page 194.

Action Steps Women Can Take

- Examine your attitudes about intimacy and whether you have sent conflicting messages to your partner.
- Initiate or participate in an open discussion of the emotional health of the relationship.
- Reward any open expression of honesty, vulnerability from your partner.
- Seek counseling for your own issues if needed or with your partner if appropriate. See page 203 for options.
- Be on the lookout for small expressions of willingness to change and reward those.
- Tell your partner what intimacy means to you and how you came to that view.
- Learn techniques to forgive and restore intimacy when that is needed, not just "kiss and make up." Remember forgiveness is not something you do for someone else. It is something you do for yourself.
- Be sensitive to signs of willingness to reconcile in times of conflict. Move toward him, not away.
- If you feel you cannot be heard without an argument, write your feelings in a letter, apologizing at the top for the hurt it may cause.
- If your partner already demonstrates a good model in this area, tell him directly.

Keeping your balance

On the scale below put a ^ mark where you think you are in your understanding of sex and intimacy and another ^ where you would like to be and will work toward.

|--|

I could use some improvement in my understanding of sex and intimacy	I have a very healthy understanding of sex and intimacy

"Anger is the one emotion that we learn early."

LESSON 4
WORKING ON OUR RELATIONSHIP SKILLS

Before we begin this section, just a reminder: As we have said before, it may seem sometimes we are overgeneralizing about the characteristics we observe in men. It is true that many men have communication and relationship skills that equal or surpass those of women. But, generally speaking, the behaviors we are discussing in this book faithfully describe what is reported by men in our discussion groups and seminars.

I like to "spill the beans" as early as possible. Bottom line: if you want to be successful in ALL relationships, the best thing you can do is to make the other person feel heard and spend time with them. If you already do that perfectly, you may skip the rest of the chapter. Otherwise, read on.

There's a disturbing revelation in Dr. John Gottman's book *The Seven Principles for Making Marriage Work.*[1] At about the age of 7, boys tend to stop playing with girls and pursue more violent activities with other boys, paying less and less attention to relationships. Think about the implications of that. This means that at a very early age, boys (for whatever reason) have not only started down a path of less attention to relationships, but have also begun to focus more and more on violent behavior. Over a lifetime, this can impact everything from connection with a partner to communication and relationship maintenance at work. As a boy, we get the message that relationship stuff is "girly." This obviously changes in adulthood because in our Men in Balance™ survey, 65% of men say they feel isolated in their personal life, and 67% would like to be better able to open up and talk with other men about personal issues.[2]

Anger is Okay

Of course some of men's tone deafness in relationships is benign, but as we have noted before, men sometimes have difficulty expressing emotions--*with the exception of anger*. This is the one emotion that we learn early and seems to be universally allowed/encouraged for men and boys. The result is that we overuse this emotion and fail to develop our use of others (e.g. empathy). Consequently, the risk is that we may become one-dimensional in our emotional makeup, and, as a result, miss out on the fruits of close relationships and fail to learn key skills such as conflict resolution and collaboration. An important note here: If you are having serious anger issues or your partner has expressed concern about your expression of anger, get help. This is not likely something you can fix by yourself. Start with some books about anger management, then get some counseling. Unmanaged or unmanageable anger can be a sign of untreated depression, which is anger turned inward. A competent counselor can tell you if this is true for you. If you don't know already, you need to learn the source of the anger.

Honesty in Conversation

Our clumsiness in relationships may cause us to have difficulty fully representing ourselves in conversation, especially with women. There are two reasons for this: First, as noted earlier, we tend to protect women from our negative feelings. Secondly, because we generally believe women have better conversation skills than we do, we default to the position of minimal interaction as our (inadequate) defense. We emotionally shut down and minimally participate in the discussion. As you might expect, this can cause significant problems in close relationships.

Think about your last disagreement with your partner. How did it end?

1) With anger and hostility that seethed over a day or more?
2) With calm discussion about the issue and a mutually agreed-upon resolution?
3) With the issue being swept under the rug for the moment?

Unless it was successfully resolved, chances are it is still a "live issue" and is causing distance between you and your partner. Enough of these instances, and the distance is difficult to overcome, so we end up with jaded, joyless relationships or open hostility and resentment. Ideally, we want to live without expectations—as impossible as that sounds. But as my former pastor, Dr. Jody Seymour, says, "An expectation is a resentment waiting to happen."

How much better would your relationship be if you could learn and consistently use good negotiation and conflict resolution methods? This is probably the most difficult work of any relationship, and I submit it is much more difficult for men. Our culture does not encourage us to negotiate solutions. Rather, it encourages us to win – – sometimes at all cost. (See the Lesson on **Competition**.)

So, we may win the battle but lose the relationship. I once knew a salesman who insisted on being technically right in any discussion, even with a prospect, and his sales tanked. As my counselor friend Philip Loydpierson says, you can choose to be right or you can choose to have a relationship.

Why don't we know how to do this?

It is a shame that our public education system does not place more emphasis on the importance of relationship problem-solving and negotiation. As a result, neither men nor women feel totally confident about successfully addressing the multiple issues in intimate relationships. And it seems that since so little emphasis is placed on this for men in particular, we mistakenly assume this is not an important skill for us to have or teach to our sons.

In recent years, the landscape has decidedly changed where communication and relationship skills in marriage are concerned. I hear more and more men saying that their partner has left them or threatened to leave because of their poor communication skills or lack of expression. Or their partner feels empty and deprived in the relationship because they want more connection. Often, men struggle with what to make of that request. Our response is to make valiant efforts to be better listeners, thinking that if we can just listen to all of her problems and offer solutions, things will settle down. Not likely. Women rightfully expect us to simply and fully interact with them, share our feelings and empathize with their feelings instead of disregarding their feelings as illogical or unimportant. (See the section on **Intimacy**). When the problems reach this stage, usually couples are seeking counseling for what they describe as a "communication" problem. More likely, it is a relationship problem that men feel hopelessly unable to fix, which adds to their frustration.[3]

Good news! There is also a lot of evidence that children from families that make valuing relationships with each other a priority tend to avoid some of the problems normally associated with children growing up, especially teenagers.

Consequences

What I'm suggesting here is that, as men, we tend to settle for shallow connection with our partners, our families, and others. So we end up with relationships, including marriages, that are far from fulfilling.

Also, because of our clumsy or absent expression of our needs to our partner, we tend to get angry and resentful that our needs are not being met, feeling that she is *withholding* the granting of our needs. It may seem this is a deliberate action on her part, but the fact is we may be expecting her to read our mind and respond to our needs--*even though we haven't voiced them*! (There are some co-dependent women who will try to read our minds routinely and it might feel good at first, but it is generally unhealthy.) Reminder: The only way to get love or affection is to offer it.

Ironically, at the same time we are accusing.her of withholding, we may be failing to provide her with deep interaction and a way of relating that would make her feel valued in the relationship--and therefore willing to give us what we need. And so a downward spiral begins which detours through a counselor's office on the way to divorce court. How much simpler and more fulfilling if we could truly learn to listen empathically to each other. By the way, voicing our needs appropriately encourages her to do the same!

A reader of our newsletter recently offered that to resolve conflict, she and her husband agree to let each other speak uninterrupted for 2 minutes each. Then after several cycles, each tries to summarize the other's position. Not bad.

Meadow Reports

In her relationship seminars, consultant Alison Armstrong talks about women needing to provide a "meadow report" when they reunite with their man at the end of the day--which is likely to frustrate him. It is as if a woman has visited a beautiful meadow recently (think metaphorically here) and insists on reporting on every tree and flower and animal she has seen because that level of detail is significant to her. Meanwhile her partner restlessly waits to hear some *problem he can solve*. Of course, there is no problem, so he may wonder why she gushes all this unusable information--since he sees his "job description" primarily as problem solver. (The report might also be about shopping, girlfriends, gossip, people at work, etc.) This tendency on the part of women to broaden the conversation is different from men who often tend to narrow the conversation.

I remember when my oldest daughter came home from her first few weeks at college and she began to tell me about the problems with her roommate. I offered, "So have you tried....." She said, "Dad, I don't need you to fix it, I just need you to listen." Ouch.

Men who are successful in their intimate relationships understand that her need for dialogue about the details of her day is an important part of her make-up and part of expressing her wish to connect more deeply. We are wise to acknowledge, accept, and value it.

New Role

We must see our role as more than a problem solver and try to become less task-driven. Our tendency to want to solve a problem gets in the way of our truly listening to what she says, and usually listening is primarily what she wants and expects. But we try to find the *problem* in what she said and offer a solution. While this may be a noble gesture, it is typically not what she expects or wants. So once again we get labeled as someone who cannot listen or is simply not interested.

If we can learn to truly listen with interest and empathy, it can be magic. Yes, there are gender differences in the things we focus on in conversation, but we need to make an effort to get closer to each other by trying to understand what the other person values and emphasizes. Hint: If you're looking for something to *do* during this time, just remember that your assignment is to listen, make her feel heard. That is what you are to DO. It will help if you can show some interest also, but keep in mind she likely isn't expecting you to remember all of this, much less do anything about it. (Whew! That's a relief!) If you're still confused, say something like, *"You've shared a lot of information with me. Is there something you need other than for me to just hear it?"* The point is to stay with *her* agenda, not yours—and relax and enjoy her communication with you.

Just one more note: It is important to give up any romantic notions that we are supposed to be in lockstep with our partner in communication or thinking. That's impossible, since we are two totally separate people. And this sort of thinking interferes with a realistic, practical approach to the relationship.

False Bravado

As men, it does not come easy for us to admit failure. Success is the golden grail and the only acceptable outcome. This has been drilled into us since we were toddlers. So, it may be difficult for us to acknowledge that we have a communication problem or that we need to work on our relationship skills, especially if we are getting along fine at work or with our buddies. So our approach may be denial and false bravado. In other words, we not only deny we have a problem and charge ahead as though nothing is wrong, we disregard the importance of communication and relationship skills with statements that tend to discount their value *("That's just too soft and mushy")*. It just doesn't seem to fit our definition of masculinity.

Impact on Our Career Path

Poor relationship skills can sometimes torpedo our career path, resulting in being passed over for promotion and, in some extreme cases, being fired. My partner and I have coached many executives who have been successful for years, especially in technical areas, but then suddenly are fired because of relationship or communication issues. This comes as a total shock to these people because they have never been told they have a problem. Suddenly, the bad habits they have developed over a lifetime reach a tipping point in a specific situation, and it results in a serious enough incident to cause them to lose their job. Or the cumulative weight of bad habits and years of poor communication simply becomes difficult to ignore. The outcome is the same.

So one lesson men can learn is the importance of open communication and what I call win-win conversations, conversations in which both parties get what they want (for the most part) and leave the conversation feeling valued, whole and intact, and even encouraged. Please don't read this as "playing nice" or being artificially accommodating. It is *much* deeper than that. I talk more about that in the next chapter. (There is also more on this in my book, *(having) Better Conversations,* available on Amazon.)

Teach the Children Well

As men, we also need to be thinking about the messages we're transmitting to our children, especially our sons. The model of masculinity we present to them will likely be adopted pretty much undiluted unless we are just clueless, in which case they may vow they will *never* behave like us.

The way we treat their mother will likely become the way they eventually treat their life partner. If we are dismissive of her input, argue with her intuitive approaches, disregard her wishes and do what we want regardless, we are sending the message to our sons that the input of our partner, their mother, is not important, and it is "manly" to ignore it. Further, we send the message that she is simply an obstacle to getting what we want. It is important to present a healthy, viable relationship model to our sons. Maybe by doing this, we can begin to break the cycle of male-female misunderstanding that has existed for generations.

And I feel the need to challenge Paul in Ephesians 5:22 when he says, “Wives submit to your husbands as to the Lord.” Sometimes this is used as a rule for “Christian” marriage. Even taking into the different culture in which that was written, today’s women think and act for themselves, as they should. But the rigid, literal interpretation of this scripture can be deadly to marriages today. I wish he had said, “Wives, partner with your husbands. And husbands, respect your wives.”

Our Relationship with Men

While we often settle for unsatisfactory relationships with our partner because of our poor relationship skills, this is exponentially more likely in our relationships with other men. We typically don't think of our relationships with men as having much to offer us. In fact, we might see other men as competitors, much as the caveman would have seen another man as a competitor for food and sustenance.

It is disappointing that our conversations with other men are typically limited to sports, sex, and occupation. Our first question when we meet another man, in fact, is typically about what he does for a living. This helps us size up the threat he represents and unless something causes us to pursue the discussion further, we are likely to switch the topic to sports or some “masculine” thing we might have in common. Or we limit the chatter to inconsequential small talk. The point is that the conversation is shallow and never gets into emotional areas or how either of us feels about anything.

It reminds me of an incident that was described in one of our sessions: The participant reported that the night before, he and his wife had visited another couple. After dinner, the men went to the garage while the women stayed in the kitchen cleaning up. The conversation in the garage was mostly benign and very little of substance was exchanged. On the ride home, his wife asked, "What did you guys talk about?" He responded that not much was said and gave no details. "Did he not tell you they are getting a divorce?" she asked incredulously. Of course, he had to say that no such discussion had taken place.

This is a great example of how little substantive information men tend to share with each other as opposed to how women readily share personal details. In fact, I have often said that men can spend an entire weekend together on a fishing or hunting trip and know very little about each other's lives when they return Sunday night. By contrast, women can spend a lunch together and learn almost everything that is going on with each other– – while talking over each other enthusiastically. The result is that women tend to more easily form close bonds which provide a network of support that is available when they need it. Men, on the other hand, tend to be very slow to open up to one another personally. Consequently, when we have a difficult situation, we find ourselves with no one we can talk to. While we may pretend this is okay, the fact is we would love to have someone with whom we can open up and share, as confirmed in our online survey. In our survey 62% of men say they would like to be in a small group with other men.[4]

I believe this is one of the main reasons Men in Balance™ has succeeded. The small group gives men a safe place to talk openly in a confidential environment about things that are troubling them in their personal lives or relationships. Most men see this as an unheard-of opportunity to open up to other men in a trusting environment, and they quickly see the value of having such supportive, non-judgmental relationships.

Incidentally, when I ask men whether they have another male friend to whom they feel close enough to talk with intimately, many times they will say they do. But when I press them for who this person is, they will say it's a college roommate from years ago or a friend who has moved away. Yet they feel sure this person would respond quickly if he was needed, even coming for a visit. Not to say it can't happen, but given our reluctance to open up to another man, much less our willingness to admit failure or vulnerability, it seems pretty unlikely we will talk to this person on any sort of regular basis or maintain any sense of closeness.

For me the value of having close relationships with men we can trust is a no-brainer. The fact is we need these connections just as much as our partners and not having them takes a toll on our personal lives. In our survey, nearly half of the men (46%) said they have NO close male friends in whom they could confide, yet most said they would like to be better able to open up and talk to other men.[5]

Someone has said (I wish I could remember who) that a good test for men and male friendships is this: Can you name the six men your wife would likely call as pall bearers for your funeral?

On a personal note, there are several men I am close to. I treasure these connections because we can talk about anything, including our own weaknesses, fears, and personal inadequacies as well as our successes. (Notice the high *emotional* and high trust content.) But these few relationships did not come easily. They came after testing the waters with guys to see how willing they were to talk about more substantive things.

One last note: If we do not have fulfilling relationships other than our marriage, we are probably placing a lot of pressure on our wife or partner to meet almost all our emotional needs. That is not fair to her and can be draining and tiring for her to accommodate.

Summary

It is never too late to begin focusing more on relationships. They are the glue which binds us to each other as humans. They require intellectual honesty, emotional honesty and lots of cultivating and tending to. But they provide the connection we must have to be all that we can be, as the Army says.

The Balanced Approach

We don't need to re-invent ourselves, but we do need to pay more attention to developing and maintaining relationships.

KEEPING YOUR BALANCE

On the scale below put a ^ mark where you think you are in your care for relationships and another ^ where you would like to be and will work toward.

|---|

I could use some improvement in my handling relationships

I have a very good track record with relationships

Soul-Searching Questions

- How would you rate yourself in terms of overall communication within your personal relationships? How could improving your communication improve relationships?
- Have you been guilty of failing to share information or feelings with your partner out of a need to protect her?
- Do you have close male friends with whom you regularly confide? How comfortable are you expressing affection for other men, through hugs, empathic statements, etc.?
- Would you be comfortable asking your partner for feedback about how you interact with her and where improvement is needed?
- Have you been aware of treating your daughter(s) differently from your son(s)? Are you okay with the messages that may send?
- What can you do to improve your relationships generally, especially difficult ones and certainly the relationship with your partner?
- What about relationships with women at work? How could you improve them?
- Are you involved in an affair? Have you calculated the potential cost to your marriage? To your family? To your career? Are you willing to have this behavior end your marriage? What need is the affair really fulfilling? Hint: it is not sex.

Action Steps Men Can Take

- If you answered yes to having an active affair, end it now. It is unlikely this can end well. If you are unhappy with your marriage, get counseling or other help or get out of the marriage. Life is too short to do this to each other.
- Seek out a counselor or trusted mentor and focus on relationship work. The payoffs, spiritual, personal and professional can be huge.
- Ask your wife for a "report card" on how you are doing relating to her and your children. DO NOT allow yourself to get defensive. Just listen, then decide where you can make changes. Keep a record of your efforts, successes.
- Focus on listening intently in all your relationships, starting with those at home and work. Paraphrase what you hear for clarity. Then ask if you got it right before moving on.
- Next time you are in a conversation with another man, instead of only talking about sports or the job, ask a question such as "*What kinds of things have you learned in your marriage?*" or "*What have you found helpful in dealing with teenagers*?" The goal is to take the conversation to a deeper level.
- Focus for several days on one relationship. REALLY try to better understand that person and their thoughts, needs.
- Record your commitments on the Personal Action Plan on page 194.

Action Steps Women Can Take

- Be patient with your partner's attempts to talk about feelings. Don't interrupt or finish his sentences. Paraphrase what you hear.
- Ask him to identify feelings, not just what he thinks. Be patient. This may be hard for him.
- In this conversation, do not appear smug or intimidating. Keep your voice soft, inviting. Hold his hand. Don't judge or correct what he says.
- Be honest with him about how you feel about his behaviors, especially anger or any hints of violence.
- Reassure him you are his friend on this issue, willing to help. But end the discussion when he says to. Go slowly.
- Ask questions to clarify what he says, but don't offer opinions unless he asks.
- If your partner decides to take the risk of being vulnerable and expresses his deep emotions (fears, anxieties, etc.) to you, treat them with respect. Don't use them as a weapon to further wound him.
- Remember that praise is a big motivator for change in many men.
- If your partner already demonstrates a good model in this area, tell him directly.

How men get wounded….

Below are some of the ways men get wounded early in life. These wounds affect your life in multiple ways, especially in relationships.

- Death of a parent
- Divorce of parents
- Bullying
- Physical abuse
- Sexual abuse
- Witnessing a traumatic event
- Shaming by teacher, parent or friend(s)
- Accident or disabling event
- Serious violation of trust by a trusted friend
- (Please add any others that might have affected you.)
- ____
- ____
- ____

It is important to learn how these events have affected your actions or beliefs. If you have not successfully worked through the trauma, please get counseling. Your life can be so much more fulfilling. I know this from experience. Jot down below any commitment you are willing to make in this regard.

____

____

"At work, we get rewarded for being competitive but when we come home, we are told we should stop this behavior."

LESSON 5
WHY OUR FOCUS ON COMPETITION IS INCOMPATIBLE WITH RELATIONSHIPS

Being in competition with your partner is not only unhealthy, it is dangerous and pointless.

You may be saying, "Me? In competition with my wife? Ridiculous." Yet most of us do this to some degree. As men, we are programmed to be competitive, almost from birth. Winning is important. Crushing the opponent is better. That works on the sports field, but not at home. Have you found yourself guilty of any of the following?

- Trying to win an argument with your wife at all costs
- Controlling the agenda on family conversations

- Correcting your partner or others on minor details
- Interrupting or talking over your partner or others
- Insisting on having the last word

What's a man to do?

At work, we typically get rewarded for being competitive except on teams, but when we come home, we are told we should stop this behavior--which is as natural to us as breathing? The answer is: YES. Granted, that is a tall order. But competition with someone in an intimate relationship kills closeness, damages trust and shreds some basic notions about intimacy. How can she feel snuggly toward someone who just slammed a winning volley at her expense?

What is the alternative? Collaboration and cooperation. That demonstrates unity, not one-upmanship. It means being on the same side of the negotiating table working to solve a problem common to both of you. Making the *problem* the opponent instead of each other.

Maybe some comparison of potential conversational phrases would help:

I think this is what we ought to do.

vs.

What ideas do you have about solving this problem?

You are dead wrong about that. Here's why...

vs.

I see that differently. Can we talk about it?

Here are the facts about this.

vs.

How do you see this?

You're not being logical about this.

vs.

I'm interested to learn how you came to that point of view.

I'm sure you can see the difference in the phrases above. The second options are much less arbitrary and final-sounding. They are much more collaborative and problem-solving, implying some willingness to be influenced. I have heard guys say these responses sound wimpy. It does take some adjustment. It is critical to learn which phrases open and extend a conversation and which phrases close it down.

Maybe an actual example is in order: Have you ever caught yourself keeping score with your partner on who did what? Who did the most housework or some other chore? Sometimes it is more subtle such as outdoing each other in conversations with others, scoring "points" at the partner's expense. ("I tried to tell her the right way to do that.")

A magic phrase almost always: "I'm interested in you you see this."

Why Collaboration?

The reasons to be collaborative in a close relationship are obvious, I hope. The question is: Why, as men, is that approach less natural or even acceptable for most of us? In other words, why is that approach not always our *default* choice? We are simply not conditioned to operate that way in our culture. In fact, just the opposite. Being forceful and definite seems to be part of our DNA. Even in everyday negotiation at work, we can get criticized if we "leave money on the table" or "don't have a winning strategy." Winning isn't just a good thing, it's the only thing, presumably said legendary Coach Vince Lombardi.

Define Winning

This brings us to a serious question: What is winning? Is winning crushing the other person? Getting your way? Prevailing in the argument? Or is it demonstrating that you value the relationship above ANY issue that might come up? Is it being so concerned about the other party, that you put your needs on hold while you honestly try to hear the other person's needs or concerns? Is it going for a win-win solution? An emotionally intelligent definition of winning rearranges priorities in a way that makes sense. (Incidentally, in negotiation, there are two negotiables: terms and relationship. If you are never going to see that person again, then it is safe to go for the best terms possible. But if you have to live with that person, relationship trumps terms.)

Does it sound wimpy and mushy to you to be collaborative? Even vulnerable? Does it go against everything you have been taught about being a man? That is very possible. In that case, you might decide a) you've got work to do, or b) that's not something you can/will do. To a lot of men, this feels like wholesale giving in to your partner/opponent. Wimping out.

Are women more collaborative?

There is a fair amount of research that suggests that women are more naturally collaborative/cooperative than men.[1] That makes sense. For most of human history women for the most part had to negotiate to get their needs met because, typically, they were dependent on the generosity of men who held the power. So maybe that is why it seems "unmanly" for men to adopt this approach.

Unless you are a cave man, collaboration seems to work better in today's environment of power sharing and joint decision-making. It is just more courteous and gentlemanly and the right thing to do at work or at home. As for concern about appearing unmanly, I submit that far more people (of either gender) find this collaborative approach more appealing than not.

As for collaboration in the board room, women have made dialogue more inclusive and less abrasive.[2] Their communication skills and risk aversion are credited with heading off costly decisions while inspiring more studied, deliberate approaches. An executive friend of mine calls this "going fast by going slow," meaning that decisions made without everybody's buy-in often are not sustainable and tend to come unraveled.

Will you change?

Here's the question: Do you feel the need to remodel your communication style to lower the "competitive" voltage? Not everyone needs to work on this, but my experience is that all of us can improve our collaboration skills and the communication that goes with them. *Managers as Facilitators* suggests that collaboration is connected directly to successful leadership.[3] If you are ready to give this serious consideration, study the questions below and look over the resources in the back of the book.

Just as an FYI: There are professional instruments which measure competitiveness. Counselors or consultants can put you in touch.

Another failed relationship?

It is worth asking whether you have had multiple relationships that all ended the same way. She did or did not do X or she ignored your need of Y. Whatever. It is important to ask what your role was in the breakup. It is doubtful that multiple women ALL had the same problem. Perhaps the problem is something *you* are doing or not doing. Perhaps competing without being aware of it, perhaps something else. Nonetheless, it is worth an honest investigation. This is how we learn to truly love.

And in a discussion with your partner, if you are harboring thoughts of "I need to win this one" you will never get to the point of making her feel loved and cherished. That's sad because you will be missing most of what she has to offer.

Summary

As men, almost from birth, we are conditioned to be competitive. We get rewarded for this in sports and usually at work. But competition does not work in close relationships and if we "compete" with our partner to the point of needing to prove ourselves, we damage intimacy. Being more collaborative requires us to abandon some ideas about competitiveness. Not everything is a sports game to be won. Winning may need to be defined differently. The language we use is a good barometer of the competitive messages we are sending.

The Balanced Approach

It is expected that we will be competitive on the sports field, but we should look for and try to get rid of any evidence of that in our close relationships. Sometimes blaming our spouse can be a form of competition ("I'm right about things more often than she is").

Soul-Searching Questions

- Have you found yourself knowingly trying to "win" arguments with your spouse/partner?
- Do you feel "wimpy" or "unmanly" using collaborative/power sharing approaches?
- How do competitive tactics harm close relationships? Have you experienced this?
- Do you agree that "winning" needs to be re-defined? How would you define it in your important relationships?
- Have you been guilty of damaging relationships in your attempts to win?
- Have you been the victim of a competitive, heavy-handed approach? How did it feel?
- Do you feel hurt or angry if someone else's idea wins over yours? Why?
- At work, have you ever "won the battle but lost the war?" What happened?
- In what areas are you fiercely competitive?

Action Steps Men Can Take

- Ask your partner for feedback on this issue, and listen patiently for the response.
- Ask one or more trusted associates at work for feedback about your style. Include a female.
- Get a book or video that deals with collaboration or communication style. Or get yourself tested by a professional
- Honestly ask yourself where you got your ideas of winning and losing? Are you willing to change them?
- Why is competition bad for relationships? What do you need to do differently?
- Define for yourself: What is a good definition of winning?
- Invite your partner to call out incidents where competition may be creating conflict in the relationship.
- Every negotiation includes elements of emphasis on relationship or terms. Winning on terms that are too harsh will damage a relationship.
- Record your commitments on the Personal Action Plan on page 194.

Action Steps Women Can Take

- Discuss this with your partner. Ask if he is okay with your pointing out when he could be more collaborative, inclusive.
- Read up on this topic and share your research with your partner.
- Talk to a trusted friend about this topic (do not criticize your partner to someone else).
- Keep a diary of your own comments that are less than collaborative.
- Be aware when you feel competition is happening in conversation with your man. Talk about it later.
- In putting your ideas forward, focus on the win-win possibilities (vs. tearing down the opponent).
- Don't just drop the issue when there is some disagreement; instead, explore your man's reasoning behind the position he is taking.
- Keep in mind he has been conditioned since youth to be competitive.
- If your partner already demonstrates a good model in this area, tell him directly.

Defining Winning….

Winning will need to be defined differently in different situations. Here are some guidelines for developing win-win outcomes:

- Must be custom to each situation
- Must be collaborative, include all parties
- Must be sustainable over time
- Must be fair to all
- Must be flexible as conditions change
- Must be realistic and practical
- Must share power appropriately
- Must leave all parties feeling whole, satisfied
- Need not be equitable, simply agreed

"Work can become a refuge from problems at home."

LESSON 6

WHY OUR FOCUS ON CAREER ROBS US OF CONNECTION

In the ongoing survey at Men in Balance™, a surprising number of men (33%) said they consider themselves workaholics. Another large group (68%) said they bring the frustrations of work home with them, check email frequently at home or otherwise are "on duty" at home. The majority (62%) said they enjoy their work and that time can slip away from them when they are working.[1]

These figures are not very different from other surveys which report similar results. As men, we enjoy our work. It gives us significance and meaning. It draws on our strengths of productivity, leadership, purpose, and results, but it can expand and take over our lives as well. It can become a refuge from problems at home, relationship issues, and intractable problems in our personal lives. Our survey shows that 70% of men feel a lot of pressure to provide well for their family and more than a third have had conflict with their partner over the number of hours they work.[2]

One complicating factor is that sometimes men allow themselves to be defined by their career—to such an extent that if they are fired or retire, they feel they have lost their identity. (See the chapter on ***How Our Failure to Develop Our Whole Selves Leaves Us Incomplete.***) I was told by one man that he spent his working hours at the library for more than a week to keep from telling his wife he had lost his job. Then there's the legendary story about former president Lyndon Johnson who, when he retired to his farm, missed tracking world events. So he had his workers keep a spreadsheet on every hen's egg production and the totals by day and month. Old habits linger.

Two-career households create their own problems. Some men feel threatened if the partner makes more than he does, for example. But also, there is the question of whose career takes precedence if a move is indicated because of a promotion or company relocation. These times call for an openness and flexibility about roles and especially who is the breadwinner (whose salary is more important) and what is implied by that. Could you, for example, see yourself as a stay at home father? Or taking the main responsibility for child rearing and household activities? These topics demand real and genuine dialogue between partners, the kind of dialogue possible only if the communication channels are clear and you are confident about your role in the relationship.

Work to live?

It comes around sooner than you think. Suddenly you have logged 15 or 20 years in your career perhaps without intentionally planning your future. It is important to know how work fits into your life. I'm sure you've heard that often at 40 to 50 years old, many men enter what has been labeled a "Mid-life Crisis." This is a well-documented phenomenon. The symptoms typically include disillusionment with work and personal life. You realize you are not going to be president of the company or get rich, you haven't planned properly for retirement, or your skill set may be rusty. And things aren't going well at home. There are incessant demands for a higher standard of living. The teenage kids are impossible. There isn't much intimacy any more. And you're feeling a "spiritual vacuum"--a sort of cynicism about life and what it is supposed to be about. (See **Introduction.**)

Yes, work can be very rewarding--seductively so. It gives us meaning and purpose and is a real stimulant to our creativity and sense of well-being. But like anything else, it needs to be kept in balance. In an interview on Men in Balance Radio, Davidson Basketball Coach Bob McKillop notes that for him career and spirituality go hand in hand and a strong spirituality is good for your career. (See ***How Our Failure to Develop Our Whole Selves Leaves Us Incomplete.***)

Even if you aren't in the "crisis" stage of feeling negative about your life, failing to keep this exciting occupational calling of yours proportionately in balance with the other elements of your life can be a problem. Missing the kids' sports events, birthday parties, etc., takes a toll on relationships with your wife and children. Missed dinners with the family or working weekends or while on vacation also begins to take the oxygen out of a marriage.

If you have gotten unpleasant feedback at home about the number of hours you work, it's probably time for a re-evaluation. Work can be addictive, and much like alcohol or drugs, it can take us away from family and become a source of imbalance in our lives.[3] Not tending to relationships along the way has consequences. It is worth noting that there are some companies which emphasize Family in their core values, expecting employees to make family a priority because that is good for business. More importantly, YOU can make it a priority.

Empty Nest

While it may be hard to imagine it happening to you, many men find too late that the kids are away at college and they are face to face with a wife they barely know because of the demanding requirements of work and raising a family. The "empty nest" syndrome is real and a lot of men make poor decisions at that time by looking for excitement in a younger woman, a racy car and a different lifestyle, sometimes ditching all they have worked for. It is easy to blame all those who have taken you for granted, especially the wife. It may sound crazy, but our goal should be to *never* place blame. Placing blame is living in the past and is a waste of time. It also suggests we consider ourselves better than the person we are blaming and that we see ourselves as flawless. You might need counseling to deal with this life passage.

Are you aligned? With what?

Pat Morley, in his book, *Man in the Mirror,* talks about climbing the ladder of success only to realize the ladder has been leaning against the wrong wall.[4] In other words, some thoughtfulness and discernment is needed to make sure your values are not being compromised or lost along the way, that your partner is on board with your life direction, and that your emotional and spiritual needs are aligned with your career goals.

Like it or not, you are a spiritual being, not to be confused with a religious being, and your psyche is at its best when you share your abilities by helping others instead of blindly accumulating more stuff or putting in more hours. If your life is consumed with selfish ambition, there is little time for generosity and its psychological rewards. Somewhere along the way, you will become aware that, as humans, we find our true purpose outside of ourselves, seeing needs and responding to them, having an awareness of a larger purpose to our lives. That is what our spiritual nature is about.

This might be a good time to connect integrity to spirituality. Having a strong sense of integrity as a core value can keep you from straying into undesirable areas. To always be what you say you are is the goal. Integrity comes from the same root as integer, meaning "one." Oneness with yourself is a goal worth pursuing.

What's Ahead for You?

I know some of these concepts can sound soft and "mushy" or even trite, but I have seen so many men go through this cycle that I ask you to consider factoring this idea into your thinking: Without a larger purpose and commitment, life can seem meaningless. Without a moral compass to keep us on track, we can drift into behaviors we can't imagine. We can lose sight of the simple yet essential things in life that really matter and bring us lasting pleasure. Whether you attend church or not, whether you believe in God or not, you need spiritual grounding to your life. Otherwise, as one of the Men in Balance™ participants said, you feel like you are going through the motions in life with little joy and purpose. Not good.

Just to take this a step further: Not only are you a spiritual being, it is important for you to be the spiritual leader of the family, working with your partner to teach children that life has a larger purpose and their future will be more rewarding if they seriously develop that side of themselves.

You've heard the saying that no man has ever claimed on his deathbed that he wished he had spent more time at work. Facing our mortality has a way of bringing priorities into focus. At 30 you can change your future; at 50 it's a lot harder. If you are retired, you can find fulfillment offering yourself as a mentor to your son or son-in-law or others, sharing what you have learned along the way.

Some questions to ask yourself:

- What gives my life meaning, real meaning? Will that change when I retire?
- Are my relationships in working order? What has damaged them?
- Do I feel I am in a race for things with little lasting value?

Here's the point I want you to get from all this: Yes, your career is supremely important in your life. Yes, achievement in your career is very rewarding. But if that is primarily what you focus on in your life, you will have missed a lot. You will seem one-dimensional, especially to your partner who longs for deeper connection with your true and best self. Learning that you have neglected this part of yourself is the definition of mid-life crisis—it is your primal spiritual nature crying out for something more, something lasting, something that brings real meaning and purpose to life. (See ***Lesson 10 How Our Failure to Develop Our Whole Selves Leaves Us Incomplete***)

Summary

As men, career is doubtless very important to us. The hard work we do is a gift to our family. It is important for us to feel appreciated for this effort. On the other hand, we can let work get out of control and cause us to shortchange our family and miss out on closeness with our partner. When we receive feedback that career has overgrown its boundaries, we need to rein it back in before our marriage and family relationships are put at risk. It is important to realize that life is more than career and work, in fact it is more about the vital relationships that sustain us and the contributions we can make to each other's lives. Being aware of this truth is vital.

The Balanced Approach

Career balance involves adhering to a core concept of not sacrificing your personal life or values for a job or career.

KEEPING YOUR BALANCE

On the scale below put a ^ mark where you think you are in your work/life balance and another ^ where you would like to be and will work toward.

|---|

I could use some improvement in my work/life balance

I have a very healthy work/life balance

Why It's Called Work

Do your best to estimate the following. If you are not currently working, use experiences from the last time you were working full time:

____ The number of hours spent at work in a typical week.

____ The number of hours spent on work at home in a typical week.

How does work impact the amount of time you are able to spend with your family? Can you quantify this?

____

How does work impact the amount of time you are able to spend on personal interests? Can you quantify this?

____

In what ways does work shape your personal friendships?

____

In what ways does work shape your non-work activities?

____

What benefits might balancing work and home life provide for you?

____

Soul-Searching Questions

- In all honesty, are you a workaholic? Are you honest with yourself about the hours you work and are you at peace with how much you work?
- Are you using work to avoid problems at home or elsewhere in your life?
- Are you and your partner in sync about work and its place in your relationship? If not, are you willing to discuss and modify that?
- Do you feel resentful having to change something you love (work) for a family which might not appreciate your sacrifice?
- Are you willing to make changes in priorities and think creatively about balancing work and family?
- How satisfied are you with your retirement plan (not the money but the personal time)?
- What personal interests, hobbies have you put on hold for the sake of the job/career?

Action Steps Men Can Take

- For 90 days, keep an accurate log of work time. Include in it any missed family events and complaints about hours you are working.
- Find an older mentor who will talk honestly with you about work/life balance issues and priorities.
- Objectively decide what changes you need to make, if any, regarding work and its place in your life.
- Discuss with your employer your work commitments and negotiate mutually acceptable changes.
- Have an open discussion with your wife concerning your feelings about work.
- Take a family vacation and rigidly avoid work-related events. No calls, emails.
- Rigidly resist answering emails/texts after hours or checking email during family time.
- Write 2 paragraphs about how you see your life after retirement. Share with your partner.
- Record your commitments on the Personal Action Plan on page 194.

Action Steps Women Can Take

- Try to initiate a loving, empathic discussion with your man about work/life balance. Talk about what YOU need instead of criticizing him.
- Get some counseling to discover ways to improve home life in spite of the work issue.
- Stop nagging about this subject. Resolve to find mutually acceptable solutions. Don't issue ultimatums.
- Develop a list of activities which will interest your partner, and schedule them (e.g. trips, visits to friends, etc.).
- Keep in mind that your partner may feel work commitments are a gift to you and you seem to be rejecting it.
- Laying on the guilt seldom works. Expressing your needs has a better chance.
- Develop other interests to consume your time putting less stress on the relationship but set some realistic boundaries for yourself about what is fair.
- Be plentiful with forgiveness and praise. Assume positive intent on his part.
- If your partner already demonstrates a good model in this area, tell him directly.

NOTES ON THIS SECTION….

"Can we overcome years of brain signals that told us one thing and now tell us another?"

LESSON 7
HOW OUR FOCUS ON INDEPENDENCE MAKES US UNAPPROACHABLE

Who are we?
As men, our earliest messages were likely about being independent, self-sufficient, tough and resilient. If we fell or got knocked down, we were expected to get back up and try again--and get it right. Even Mom would shout from the sidelines of a baseball game, "Shake it off. You can do it!"

My generation bought heavily into the John Wayne tough guy model. Not only were you to be fiercely independent, you were supposed to be fearless as well. And talk like it. Part of the persona was also to avoid showing emotion. Especially do not show weakness or even flexibility. Avoid connection. *Always* be tough. Like a rock. *Never* vulnerable. If our fathers exhibited these traits, we may have adopted them as well.

Unfortunately, those traits do not work in intimate relationships where collaboration is expected and cooperation is essential. So it happens that guys who have bought into the John Wayne "tough guy" persona might find a clash they had not expected with a partner whose expectations are very different. This model doesn't work in the office either when teamwork and collaboration are core values to be measured against. You can get labeled as "not a team player" and your days may be numbered.

I have a lot of empathy for men who find themselves in this conundrum--how to be the kind of man you were taught to be and also be tender and gentle with a partner. And while workplace managers might demand “teamwork,” they also send a clear message to be a self-starter with a bias for action and to press ahead and get things done. Be tough. Forceful. Decisive. However, you are supposed to change your personality 180 degrees when you cross the threshold of home, becoming collaborative, gentle, soft-spoken. That’s really hard.

If you’re unclear about what we are talking about, here are some illustrations and some notes about both the good and questionable implications:

Being autonomous

Good: We can make decisions for ourselves, not depending on anyone else.

Questionable: Not involving key people, especially our partner, can result in poor decisions and conflict.

Being Self-reliant

Good: We can take care of ourselves and get things accomplished on our own.

Questionable: Appearing unrealistically self-reliant can be off-putting to others, making them feel you have no need for others.

Not dependent on anyone

Good: This means we can stand alone and be our rugged selves. We make it clear we can do whatever is required.

Questionable: No one is likely to hang around waiting for a chance to help out or connect. Family members may keep their distance.

Lone Wolf

Good: You are not a burden to anyone, you take care of yourself.

Questionable: Being a lone wolf can get pretty lonely and it sends the message to stay away.

Not to be tamed or harnessed

Good: This sort of "wild spark" might inspire you to try new approaches (alone).

Questionable: Your whole persona can be sending the message that your independence matters more than relationships. No one gets close. You're seen as self-centered.

Resourceful

Good: You can find ways to get things done while others are talking about it.

Questionable: Your solution is likely incomplete unless you are a genius. The input of others can make your solution stronger. It's easy to become oversold on yourself and believe you have all the answers.

Defiant

Good: Shows bravery and willingness to take on challenging, even dangerous or threatening assignments.

Questionable: The sort of bravado required to maintain this image is tiring and disingenuous. Courage gets confused with macho behavior.

Consequences

Good: Willing to accept the consequences of choices, especially bad ones and somehow make it work.

Questionable: Appearing infallible is a barrier to interaction and collaboration. Compensating for your own self-doubt can be a full-time job.

It may be helpful to see this issue of independence on a spectrum ranging from totally independent to totally collaborative rather than an either/or problem. The goal is to move along the spectrum to more of a collaborative, power sharing approach, a place of genuine dialogue with our partners about the key issues in life. So rather than locking in to a position that seems right to us, we start with a solicitation of our partner's input. No commitment, just asking for input. Then mull it over and objectively see if her position doesn't have something to offer, perhaps a compromise position or collaborative solution suitable to both.

Can we change? Should we?

If the kinder, gentler, collaborative man is what we are asked to model at home, can we do that? Can we overcome years of brain signals that told us one thing and now tell us another? Neuroscientists in numerous studies are pretty clear that old patterns are hard to break.[1] Those neurons have carved deep ruts in our brain traveling the same path day after day for years upon years, and that has shaped us. Yet most women today are demanding qualities which would have made The Duke cringe—and likely require us to fight our brain's efforts to maintain the status quo.

Nonetheless, if we are to become more fully human and more in touch with ourselves and our families, it does seem some change is called for. The good news is Cognitive Behavioral Therapy (CBT) is replete with examples of people changing everything from their obsessive hair pulling to smoking cessation.[2] Using a disciplined approach involving small changes over time, hundreds of people now have better lives coupling this approach with good counseling. There are several good approaches on the subject listed in the resource section. There are other good therapies as well, some of which you can do for yourself.

If keeping your marriage and family isn't motivation enough to change, perhaps some deeper thinking is called for. Professional counseling is always available to help with this and there are great resources on the Internet geared to this idea of personality change (goodtherapy.com). You may not believe it, but your relationships are never going to be totally fulfilling until you have dealt with "your own stuff." This means getting to the root of problems you have carried around for life. We can't get by with "that's just me" or "that's just the way I am." A psychologist friend of mine once said, "The only time you can be yourself is when you're by yourself."

For partners, this is an area where your man can really use your tender prodding and encouragement. Reward the good behaviors you notice without criticizing the old ways. Soon some change can begin to happen. Encourage him to talk about his ideas regarding independence and manhood and how those were formed.

It is reassuring to know that when we talk about vulnerability in men, we are not talking about becoming a rag doll or totally giving up independence. We're talking about "appropriate vulnerability" for the circumstance and workable independence. And the requirements of an intimate relationship are a good crucible in which to practice becoming "a new kind of man."

Summary

Independence is very important to most men. It's usually a sign of our masculinity and our "take charge" natures. It can serve us well in a work environment but can be counterproductive at home. Being overly independent can come from resistance to sharing power. Likely our partners need us to be less "tough guy" and more tender in our dealings with them. This can sound counter to what we have been taught about being an independent male, but can make our lives and close relationships far more meaningful. The good news is that we don't have to totally give up our independence or masculinity to accomplish this. But it does require us to adopt a new way of relating to those we love.

The Balanced Approach

You can maintain a lot of independence and still be open to and solicitous of the ideas of others.

Soul-Searching Questions

- What did you learn as a child about manhood and independence? Were they appropriate lessons?
- How might the "tough guy model" inhibit closeness and openness with your partner?
- Are you genuinely willing to let yourself be more vulnerable and open with your partner? What would you do, specifically?
- What are your fears or concerns about being more collaborative? Are those concerns valid or just habit?
- Are you clear about the boundaries of independence and vulnerability?
- Can you see yourself in balance--appropriately independent and yet very relationship-minded?
- How important is it to you make some change in this area?
- What "payoff" can you see in making this change? What help do you need?

<u>Action Steps Men Can Take</u>

- Ask for feedback about this topic from your partner. Be willing to listen without getting defensive.
- Investigate CBT (Cognitive Behavior Therapy) or other therapies to learn more. Buy or borrow a book about men's issues. (See **Resource** section)
- Work on being more collaborative and less independent in decision making. Remind yourself to involve others.
- If appropriate, apologize to your partner and/or family for not being more sensitive to their needs.
- Map out a plan for change. Keep it handy (on your phone?). Chart your progress but keep it private.
- Initiate a discussion about this topic with a men's group or Sunday School class.
- Record your commitments on the Personal Action Plan on page 194.

Action Steps Women Can Take

- Engage your man in a discussion about this topic. Get him to define where he got his ideas about manhood and independence.
- Praise any change you notice that is headed in the right direction.
- Never nag, but when you are comfortable, say, "*Here's what I would like more of from you....*"
- Coach other parents to let their boys be themselves and not push kids to absorb hurt "like a man."
- Think about how your father showed independence. Is that a model you would want for your husband or son?
- Instead of starting with a complaint, try "I'm wondering if you would be willing to listen to me for a few minutes?" Then talk about your concerns in a non-accusatory way.
- If your partner already demonstrates a good model in this area, tell him directly.

Keeping your balance

On the scale below put a ^ mark where you think you are in your focus on independence and another ^ where you would like to be and will work toward.

|---|

I could use some improvement in my focus on independence	I have a very healthy focus on independence

"The habit of accumulating toys plays into our competitive nature."

LESSON 8
HOW OUR PREOCCUPATION WITH TOYS KEEPS US FROM CONNECTING

"He who ends up with the most toys wins."
How often have you heard that statement? Of course, we don't take it seriously, or do we? We compete with other male friends to acquire toys and status symbols. We make value judgments about what kind of car the neighbor drives or the Apple watch our work colleague is wearing. *(Here we are defining "toys" as all the gadgets and trinkets that we give ourselves because we feel we deserve them.)*

It is logical. Marketers push products at us constantly in the 250,000 plus commercials we typically see in a given year, let alone the hundreds of other media impressions we are exposed to. But really, must we be helpless slaves to mass marketing? Do we really define ourselves by what we *own*? Do we unintentionally allow "stuff" we have accumulated to interfere with relationships and things of substance?

I admit that I feel somewhat of a hypocrite talking about this subject because, at one time, I was obsessed with technology and having the newest of everything. I would skim the ads in the Sunday paper, then go buy myself a toy. I'm sure it was consolation for the demands of a heavy work schedule and lots of travel. I convinced myself that I "deserved" something because I had given up so much of myself for work.

Does that sound familiar? Of course, there is nothing wrong with enjoying the rewards of our work. The temptation, however, is to use our accumulated toys (ranging from the latest iPhone to a Corvette) as a scorecard for how we are doing in life. It is more concerning if we allow ourselves to compare the trinkets we have accumulated to those of our friends, especially if we feel we must soon give ourselves whatever they've recently acquired.

The Toys R Us?

The game of accumulating toys plays into our competitive nature. When you couple competition with the notion of accumulation of toys as reward for hard work, you can see how our values might get skewed. I'm sure there are many psychological reasons why we buy toys. Certainly, they give us a certain type of comfort, maybe even an artificial sense of control of our lives. And, for sure, they place us on a respectable level with our buddies. How often have you seen a group of guys at a gathering of some sort comparing gadgets?

If there is a danger in accumulating toys for their own sake, it is that we run the temptation of neglecting other critical parts of our lives. The time we spend doodling away on a gadget could be spent in helping others or in contemplating how we might improve ourselves or the world. Or just *being* with another human. Admiring or fussing over our trinkets doesn't lead us toward closer interaction with others. That may sound harsh, but I talk to a lot of men who say they feel a spiritual void in their lives, even as they are at the peak of their professional career, earning power, and accumulation of toys.

Spirituality and Toys

My favorite description of spirituality is that it *forces us to get outside ourselves.* It's hard to get outside ourselves if we are consumed with our possessions and our status symbols. But for me, finding the time to help others and build healthy relationships with other men is ***a non-negotiable life priority***. It gives me satisfaction and I believe helps me be a better person. I can't say that about my toys.

Where to find the time to do things for others? I am very aware that men already feel their time is devoured by work and family obligations, so to add another task to the list (helping others) may seem to be an impossible request. It is not something that is essential, but it is something that adds real meaning to your life. And this is the paradox of giving. Yes, it takes some of your time and, yes, it involves some sacrifice, but the rewards are plentiful. I have talked to men who have committed an hour a week to tutoring inner-city children, or mentoring recovering alcoholics, or helping rebuild a playground for a church and, to a person, they say those activities brought a new sense of purpose, peace, meaning, and fulfillment to their lives. The amazing unselfish caring for others seen routinely in disaster illustrates this.

Nothing gives us a better feeling about ourselves than helping others. And we can't do this with financial contributions as a substitute for "sweat equity." Churches and volunteer non-profit agencies are in great need of your talents. Ask your minister or someone with good community connections for suggestions where you might fit in. Or look online for agencies involved in the kind of things you enjoy or feel strongly about. Then, roll up your sleeves and enjoy the rewards of knowing you're making a difference. Don't underestimate the importance of this.

Why Bother?

The exercise analogy is probably a good one as it relates to spirituality and helping others. If you don't exercise regularly, you don't see any immediate consequences of that choice. Maybe you gain a pound or two, but no major health issues. The unforeseen consequences may take years to become fully apparent. Similarly, not having a strong spiritual grounding may not seem to be a problem until you hit a "speed bump" in your life such as divorce, or job loss, health problem, or an unexplained disenchantment with life that causes you to lose balance. It is in this time that we fall back on whatever spiritual grounding we have developed and if there is nothing there to support us, like Humpty Dumpty, we can fall off the wall and get broken. This may get labeled as a midlife crisis, which is usually more accurately described as a spiritual crisis, but the result is the same: We question the purpose of our life, and we wonder if this is all life has to offer. If you mix that feeling with some unhappiness in your marriage or home life, you have a volatile mix which can derail our lives. Our collection of toys is of little help.

I mentioned earlier that I was self-absorbed in my toys for a while. But ultimately, I found it not very satisfying. It was only when I refocused my priorities toward helping others or paying more attention to important relationships, that I began to "get it." When I started Men in Balance™ in 2007, I had no idea how rewarding and helpful it would be to see men who were struggling find a safe harbor and the chance to reorient their personal and spiritual lives, especially if they were coming off a divorce or other life trauma. The idea came out of a spiritual gifts class in which we each shared what we believed *ours and the others* gifts to be. What would a similar opportunity for you look like? *That is your assignment: To think through what brings meaning to your life and how to refocus your energy more positively by tackling that.*

Toy Etiquette

While we are on the subject of toys, just a word about etiquette. I realize our culture is changing and it is becoming more commonplace to see people fiddling with their gadgets at any time or place. However, my rule for the use of gadgets is that if there is someone else in the room to engage with, you should not be working with a gadget. We lose so much by our failure to fully engage with each other. I see teens texting each other in the same room! There is research showing that, in many cases, teens have lost the ability to carry on routine conversations, even on a job interview, and that is attributed to their dependency on texting to communicate.[1] Another interesting note: My wife says it looks bad if I take notes on my phone during a sermon or lecture, but pencil and paper are okay. The times, they are a' changin'?[2]

Bottom Line

The important thing here is to be aware of what you're giving up by becoming so enamored of your gadgets or toys. If this is taking you further away from your relationships, it's probably time to set some boundaries. If you're spending lots of time at home checking work emails or responding to work-related crises, or with your head in your latest toy, you can't be fully relating to your family and those around you. If both parties in a relationship are spending their together time this way, critical opportunities for deeper communication are lost. My suggestion is to set some boundaries for the use of gadgets and toys at home. And impose these boundaries on children as well. How about, for example, at least one "technology-free hour" each night?

I know it sounds old-fashioned, but there's a lot of spiritual nurturing to be had for both parties in our deeper caring for relationships. If we are using technology to keep us from closeness with others or to help us dodge conflict, that is certainly not healthy. We need to be totally present with our families and with our partners, engaging on multiple levels. As noted elsewhere, if you have problems in your relationship, get some help with that, but don't allow the problems (or side-stepping them) to continue to take the oxygen out of your marriage. Find ways to deal with the problems rather than use technology or other unhealthy practices as a substitute for real connection.

We Need Connection

As much as we might like to think of ourselves as "like a rock," that is not healthy. In the Simon and Garfunkel song *I am a Rock*, it is obvious this idea is a defense mechanism to avoid the pain of dealing with relationships. Even if you are having conflict with your partner at the moment, I urge you to re-examine your role in that conflict and be sure that you are totally engaged and not withdrawing. If you are not totally present with your partner, and that includes properly dealing with conflict, you can't blame her for the problems between you. As men, we are not taught to pay proper attention to the mechanics of relationships and certainly we are not trained to handle conflict properly, but it is most likely that at least half the problems in our relationships belong to us. It will be hard to solve them if our heads are buried in our toys and gadgets.

Summary

As men, sometimes we focus too much on the rewards of our hard work. We may feel entitled to special toys or trinkets that compensate us in some way for the long hours. It might never occur to us that focusing so much on our possessions gets in the way of our relationships and our spiritual nature. Interaction with others is important to our emotional health and it is a gift we can give to those we love. If we can achieve a balance between enjoying the fruits of our labor and helping others, we can have a better and more balanced life and improve our marriages and close relationships.

The Balanced Approach

Toys and gadgets are helpful and fun but must not keep us from deeply engaging with those we love.

KEEPING YOUR BALANCE

On the scale below put a ^ mark where you think you are in your focus on toys and another ^ where you would like to be and will work toward.

|--|

I could use some improvement in my focus on toys

I have a an appropriate amount of focus on toys

Soul-Searching Questions

- Honestly, are you spending too much time on toys and gadgets at home?
- Are you using toys and gadgets to avoid connection or sidestep conflict?
- Do you long for closer connections to your partner or family?
- Does others' use of gadgets bother you? Can you empathize with them?
- What toys can you give to charity and simplify your life?
- Is the attitude you have toward toys and gadgets one that you would recommend to your children?
- BIG question: What hole in your life are you trying to fill with toys?

Action Steps Men Can Take

- Put yourself and your family on a technology diet.
- Put the time you spend with your toys into a project that helps others.
- Become more active in worship or reflective meditation or find other spiritual renewal resources.
- Create a To Do list for your own spiritual renewal.
- Give half your toys to charity and simplify your life.
- Never use your gadgets when there are people around to interact with.
- Record your commitments on the Personal Action Plan on page 194.

Action Steps Women Can Take

- Encourage your man to pursue his spiritual side. Discuss that with him.
- Join him in the move away from the accumulation of toys or possessions.
- Explore some spiritually renewing activities you can do together.
- Insist on "presence time" with the family.
- Model the way by demonstrating appropriate time spent with toys and gadgets.
- Initiate a family discussion about this and set some rules.
- If your partner already demonstrates a good model in this area, tell him directly.

"It hurts to think we are failing on some important measure."

LESSON 9
OUR DIFFICULTY RECEIVING AND LEARNING FROM FEEDBACK LEAVES US ISOLATED

I'm going to start this chapter with an assignment. Using a sheet of paper folded in half, write out the things you believe your partner expects of you, then put a blank by each item. Ask for a letter grade on how you are doing on these items. Leave a couple of lines for more items to be added as needed. This "Report Card" is your To Do list for behavioral change. Ask your partner to complete it, then ask her to talk with you about any concerns and just listen without defending.

Now the tough question: Did you feel really nervous about this assignment? Are you worried that you might get really bad grades, like in school, and have a lot of explaining to do to someone--in this case, you?

Many men have difficulty receiving feedback, especially from their partner. Often, we react defensively because we know how hard we try to be good providers, fathers, and husbands. It hurts to think we are failing on some important measure.

360 Feedback

At work, you may have experienced a 360-degree feedback exercise. In this process, you receive written feedback to a prepared set of relevant performance questions, from those to whom you report, those who report to you, and those who are your peers. It's anonymous, but it doesn't take away the sting of learning some people see you as doing less than perfect work. Their feedback may include very direct comments as well as measurement indicators. Of course, you also get to rate yourself and my experience is that many people (women more than men) rate themselves more harshly than their colleagues do. We are typically not totally unaware of where we might be missing the mark. The point here is that *no matter how hard we may be trying, others may evaluate our performance differently*. Maybe we are not giving them precisely what they need. Maybe we have drifted off the job description, or maybe we are not giving 100%. At work, we are expected to submit to some form of evaluation as a means of justifying our salary. So maybe this is a good idea for home as well. I recently read an article in which both spouses renew their written contract every year with *very* specific requirements of each other.

What Gets in The Way?

Learning to receive feedback is possibly the most valuable trait you can develop. It may not be pleasant, but how else can you learn what is expected and needed from others? Feedback is a gift. But nobody is likely to continue to offer you feedback if your response is to defend your behavior. So, while it is not easy to do, it is wise to hear the feedback without defensiveness. It's possible your wife has tried to gently give you feedback and given up because of how you reacted or over-reacted to it. Ask her to try again. Think of feedback as a loving contribution to your success. Someone has risked their status with you to help you improve and become a better person. Be grateful.

So why is it so difficult for us to receive feedback from our partners? Do we believe we are perfect? Do we worry that the feedback is masking larger concerns she may have? Is our ego too fragile to learn from someone's helpful observations? Do we feel we have lost her acceptance?

(Just a note: At this point you may be asking yourself, "When do I get to give her feedback and tell her what I expect?" Just remember, this is a book for your development and deals with keeping your side of the street clean. For now, let that be enough for you.)

She Is Not Your Mom

Sometimes it might be that getting feedback from our partner is too similar to criticism we may have received in earlier days from our mom or dad. Those early attempts to instruct us also bruised our ego, particularly if they were not handled well. So when your wife does the same thing, all those memories come rushing back. We re-live the feelings we had as children or young men getting corrected and feeling a strong sense of shame, a powerful emotion. Needless to say, we will do almost anything to avoid those feelings. When we get criticism from our spouse or partner, it is natural that we would be defensive and try to deflect the incoming fire. It can seem like an attack and the body and brain gears up to defend the "fort."

If this over-reaction to feedback is something you would like to change about yourself, keep in mind:

1. Your wife is not your parent or your ex-lover or your ex-wife. She is the person closest to you and is therefore the one most aware of your shortcomings. She is also likely the one who is most interested in your success. If you could ask her, she would say that her feedback is lovingly intended to make you an even better person. She sees it as a nurturing gesture. She would probably be crushed to think you saw her comments as an attack or that she caused you pain or anxiety.

2. I'm assuming you don't want to be without her feedback, but would like it to be less painful. The pain is not a function of the words she is saying so much as it is *how you are hearing those words*. So the best option is to change the way you *react* to her feedback by not attributing a motive to her.

For example, when she says, "You're not going to wear that shirt, are you?" you quickly feel your emotions rising and you may, in fact, say something you'll later regret. You may be wondering why she is so critical. It's time for a little angel to appear on your shoulder and whisper: "Here is the chance to change the direction of the conversation. Instead of a defensive reaction, take two seconds and think what is going on. She is wanting to help you and she is probably right in her comments. To make the best of the situation, you might ask her what problems she sees with that shirt or why she does not like that shirt, paying attention to your tone of voice.[1] If you will do that, you can understand that she really wants you to look nice and be proud of you. Then you can see her comments as helpful." Thank the little angel.

Assume positive intent

In dealing with a partner, it is always good to "assume positive intent." This means that (unless she has psychological problems) you should assume she is intending good things in her actions toward you.[2] If you cannot convince yourself this is true, perhaps there is a deeper problem requiring counseling for one or both of you. But if you can objectively evaluate your feelings and listen to what she is saying, it is easier to believe she intended good things for you. There is no reason to get angry, defensive or hurt about what she said. It is only a shirt, after all, and it is really not worth a fight. So just ask her which shirt she prefers, give her a kiss, and move on. (Think about other situations where this approach could work.)

To go back to our earlier exercise, take advantage of the report card as a way of getting constructive feedback from your partner. Think of it as you would a physical checkup. You want to know as early as possible if there are danger signs that need your attention. With that approach, make the best use of that feedback by changing things that need to be changed. Keep in mind that even if you don't see your behavior as an issue, if it's a problem for her, it's a legitimate concern. (We are not talking about *her* shortcomings for the moment, only yours.)

Here is something you might be able to identify with: Sometimes in a session, one or more guys will accuse me of "taking the wife's side" of an issue. I try to assure them that my goal is to take the *right* side of the issue, favoring neither the husband nor the wife. Sometimes our years of thinking a certain way or our conditioning early in life may give us blind spots which keep us from seeing ourselves accurately as well as the implications of our behavior. If your approach is to defend yourself, punish your wife, win an argument regardless of the cost, then de-fusing a situation with kind or neutral language might seem like caving in. If you can be charitable and assume positive intent just for a moment, your life can be better. *Always* listen to the angel.

Just to belabor the point, remember that defense is a wall or fortification that you construct to protect yourself from the arrows (or bullets) of the enemy. In conflict with your spouse, it may feel, at a deep primal level, as if your life is at stake so it feels natural and necessary to “defend.” Actually, it is probably ego, your “manly” self-image that is endangered. But you can handle this!

The challenge for men is to tear down that wall—to allow the arrows or bullets to come through and know that they are not lethal, that you will survive. This is the ultimate act of vulnerability, the willingness to be “wounded” momentarily for the sake of the relationship.

Summary

Nobody likes to receive negative feedback about themselves. But if someone is willing to give us feedback, we should pay attention because there is value in it--even if it stings for the moment. If we are defensive instead of receptive, the other person is not likely to continue offering us this gift, but if we can assume positive intent about the other person's motives and believe they want the best for us, we can learn from the feedback and not feel bruised in the process. Plus, it saves a *lot* of conflict. It is important to keep our emotions under control while we mull over the feedback and plan what change is required.

The Balanced Approach

On a spectrum of "always defensive" to "never defensive," we need to move more to the direction of never defensive. Even small movement is helpful. We need not defend anything really. Hearing someone's gift of feedback is helpful to our growth.

WHY WOULD YOU BE DEFENSIVE?

Ask yourself why you are defensive on certain topics:

- Are you insecure?
- Have you had a bad experience?
- Do you have strong control needs?
- Are you a perfectionist?
- Do you lack trust in your own ideas, beliefs, values?
- Do you feel your manhood is being challenged?
- Do you have trust issues?

Soul-Searching Questions

- Do you frequently get defensive in response to comments from your wife?
- At work, do you become defensive of your ideas or comments when they are challenged?
- Can you visualize yourself almost never being defensive? Would that be a worthwhile goal?
- Do you feel you are frequently "on guard," ready to defend your actions? Where did you develop the need for this?
- Have you received feedback at work or at home that you are defensive? That is worth investigating.
- Can you separate feedback you receive from motive you might ascribe to the giver?
- What changes do you think you need to make in the area of defensiveness?

Action Steps Men Can Take

- If this is a serious problem, get some counseling for yourself.
- Really get honest with yourself about the reason you believe your partner's motive is hostile or malevolent.
- Think quietly before responding to things that make you defensive. Choose a more neutral response. Postpone responding and mull it over.
- Thank the person for their feedback (even if it is hard to do).
- Remember feedback is almost always about a behavior, not you or your character. You can change your behavior.
- Pick an issue and ask your wife for feedback about it. Resolve to listen and never defend.
- Think back about why you learned to be defensive. Who gave it? Remember that person is not in charge of your life.
- Keep a record of any fights with your spouse. Revisit the list to see if your defensiveness added to the conflict.
- Record your commitments on the Personal Action Plan on page 194.

Action Steps Women Can Take

- Apologize for causing him pain, then gently remind him that you trust his feedback and you want him to trust yours.
- Examine your choice of words and tone of voice in giving him feedback. Make it as neutral, non-judgmental as you can.
- Don't back away from offering feedback. Help him to learn to accept it.
- Forgive him for his emotional response as you try to empathize and understand his defensiveness.
- Make your feedback about behavior—what he said or did—not about attributes or character. Ask for what you want him to do, not what you want him to be.
- Use “I” statements, not “You” statements. (I have noticed....vs. You always....)
- Rehearse before delivering feedback. Keep it constructive, never personal (about his character, nature).
- Thank him for his good traits and commitment.
- If defensiveness is a problem for you also, get counseling together.
- If your partner already demonstrates a good model in this area, tell him directly.

"My wish for men is for them to pursue actively being all that they can be in their personal and spiritual life."

LESSON 10
HOW OUR FAILURE TO DEVELOP OUR WHOLE SELVES LEAVES US INCOMPLETE

We are losing the involvement and self-development race to women.

Recent statistics show for the first time in history that more women than men are graduating from college.[1] And while they are in college, women are getting higher grades than men. And as for the "glass ceiling," women are getting promotions in corporations at a pace that outclasses men. Add to that the fact that more women than men are signing up for lifelong learning classes, exercise programs, volunteer work, church leadership roles (including pastor) and you can see that there is a substantial feminine influence taking place in our society. This is not a bad thing. For example, corporation boards are learning that the feminine input may avert decisions made on the basis of ego or thoughtless aggressiveness or insensitivity.[2] There is even research that suggests that female-dominated societies are more likely to thrive.

Churches have begun acknowledging that most of the volunteers and lay people are women and have geared services, even decor, to a more feminine appeal. This has been noted by David Murrow. In his book *Why Men Hate Going to Church*, he specifically considers ways in which men might be re-engaged in church life: through giving men opportunities to discover and better use their gifts; letting men play a role in pastoral care; giving men big projects that capture their imaginations; and giving men adventure and risk in those projects.[3]

Who is involved?

Men in some areas seem to have faded into the background. I see a tendency toward less participation generally by men in family decision-making and sometimes less involvement in social issues at large (i.e. politics, civic affairs). I'm at a loss to explain this, and it is just my observation, but it seems to me that men are less often demonstrating curiosity about learning about their environment and are less often bothering to explore areas of self-development (based on what I hear in sessions with them). Most of the political meetings or change-oriented efforts I have attended recently are dominated by women. Why is that? (Do your own research on this: Next time you are at a school or political or neighborhood meeting, count the number of men vs. women.)

None of this is to diminish the amazing contributions men make in the workplace and society every day. But using indicators that are measurable such as college registrations, academic achievement, volunteer involvement and others, men seem to be falling behind women more often than not.

As men, we definitely lead women in stress and heart disease, although they are catching up. (That's not an area in which we particularly want to excel.) We have long known that men don't take care of their health as they should. Even excluding pregnancy-related doctor visits, women were 33% more likely than men to visit a doctor, although the difference decreases with age. These statistics were compiled by the Centers for Disease Control and Prevention's National Center for Health Statistics. The study also found that the rate of doctor visits for such reasons as annual examinations and preventive services was 100 percent higher for women than for men.[4]

What gets our attention?

In the conversations I have with men, I hear a frustration with expectations surrounding their new role and a confusion about what is expected. It appears that in the absence of a clearer direction, many men have defaulted to hanging back, waiting for further instructions from headquarters--wherever that is. It troubles me that this may lead to an atrophy of some of the skills and talents men are most known for and which can contribute most to families and society. For example, if men are deferring more to their spouses on household matters and family decisions, there will be some repercussions from that, one being that our input may ultimately be seen as unnecessary.

I think part of the reason we hang back is our reluctance to enter into conversations that might result in conflict, but some of it may also be due to the disorientation men are feeling about their role in today's marriage and family life. We seem to be unsure when to speak up and when to challenge, especially where our partners are involved.

By contrast, we have not given up our attention to work and career. We continue to pursue vocation vigorously and statistics bear that out.

But as for self-development, I have concerns that we are not doing our best. Some examples:

- Men are much less likely to go to counseling, believing that they should be able to "fix" their problems themselves. When they do go, it is typically the female partner's suggestion.

- By deferring to their wives more frequently, many men seem to be giving up their proxy on key family decisions and goals. So, as a result, the wife is becoming the key decision maker in the family and the spiritual leader as well, where that exists. This might be all right if we are OK with her decisions, but if we are doing this just to keep peace in the family and steer clear of conflict, that can't be good. Typically, that will build accumulated resentment, which will surface eventually.

My wish for men is that they actively pursue being all that they can be in their personal and spiritual lives. Signing up for courses, pursuing volunteer opportunities, developing new *close* relationships, seeking opportunities to help — — these are things known to make us less one-dimensional, make us more complete, and give us a greater satisfaction in life. If we choose to sit on the sidelines and let events take their course without our input, we do this at our own peril. Co-incidentally, I find a sizeable number of men dread retirement because they have failed to develop other abiding interests outside of career.

Can you fix this?

Men love to "fix things." But today's problems, especially relationship problems, don't lend themselves to an owner's manual fix-it approach. They involve much more nuanced communication skills and interpersonal agility to navigate unfamiliar terrain. They demand a committed, “all-in” attitude. Men need to excel at these behaviors. I believe if men are not seriously willing to pay attention to and learn these new required skills, they will be more and more unhappy in their marriages and perhaps see their roles as family leaders diminished.

As we have noted elsewhere, your relationships will never be at their best unless you have dealt with your own issues, some of which you have carried around since childhood. We must engage and stay engaged with our wife and family and make serious efforts to overcome whatever barriers or deficiencies inhibit our *total* involvement. We need to be energetically participating and make it clear that we are on board. This is going to mean still more time demands as we try to crowd new personal explorations into our schedules. But, like failing to exercise, ignoring this important need in ourselves can only lead to trouble. An example: Spending an hour a week proactively offering to help someone, or reading a self-help book, taking an online or physical course can produce rewards without overcrowding the schedule. The psychological reward of developing ourselves can trump any excuses we make. (See the Chapter ***How Our Preoccupation with Toys Keeps Us from Connecting***)

What's on your To Do List?

So maybe it is time to create a different kind of To Do List. This one is purely about self-development and should include whatever things you have always wanted to do but did not pursue for lack of time or energy. Taking that yoga or cooking class. Signing up to tutor kids. Learning photography or how to play a guitar. Committing to chair a church committee. Reading a self-help book. Paying attention to your spiritual self. In short, expanding your horizons beyond your current work and family obligations. In the process, you will find yourself becoming less one-dimensional and a lot more interesting and exciting to your partner. That seems like a pretty good payoff.

How counseling can help

Counseling comes in many forms: It can be a suggestion from a friend, a conversation with a pastor, or long-term therapy. My experience is that men tend to avoid going to counseling, which is like putting off that knocking noise in your car's engine until it fails. It's like they are feeling "if I don't think about it, maybe it will go away." It won't. To ease your fears a little, counseling does not have to be a "bare-all, spill your guts" kind of event. Just as you don't need a complete physical from your doctor when you're experiencing a rash, a counseling session can be minimally invasive to your psyche and tailored to your stated need. You might think of it as a personal inner journey to learn about yourself. The purpose can be simply to explore alternatives or brainstorm new options to what you are now doing, which likely isn't working. I strongly encourage you to schedule a session alone or with your wife to get help solving problems. You might start with a visit to your pastor or just doing some research. See page 203 for options.

Define the problem as best you can

Counselor Philip Loydpierson encourages men to go to a counseling session with a clear objective, even if the idea of going wasn't his. Examples might be:

- Improve communication with my children
- Overcoming or managing anger
- Solving a specific problem with my partner
- Become less defensive
- Resolve a marital standoff

"Getting my wife to read my mind and give me what I want" is not a valid topic. Ask around for the names of some good counselors or go to goodtherapy.com for suggestions. Interview them by phone before you decide. If the one you choose doesn't seem to be compatible, try another.

One more thing: I'm convinced that many relationships and marriages end needlessly and that skilled counseling could have prevented the breakup. It also can re-unite couples who have gone separate ways. Even if there are NO known problems at the moment, counseling can help you set a vision for the relationship that will serve you well in terms of ongoing maintenance. Schedule a psychological checkup just like you do your physical checkup.

I think some people avoid counseling because they worry it may bring up some divisive issues or make matters worse. Think about this: Would you like to know that your relationship can withstand the tension and discomfort of solving a thorny problem? The only way to know is to plow ahead and tackle it. Not doing so means you will always be uncertain. And likely carry around a lot of needless resentment as well.

This is fascinating: Dr. John Gottman set up a "Love Lab" to observe couples in ordinary conversation and interaction. He says he can tell within 5 minutes with 91% accuracy which couples will still be married in three years, just by observing how they treat each other[3]. That is a good argument for treating each other with love and respect at all times.

Church Stuff

As for men and church involvement, here are a few church statistics from *Why Men Hate Going to Church*:

- On any given Sunday, the audience in most churches is about 60 percent female (up from 53% in the 50's). Nationally, that's well over 13 million men AWOL from church.

- About one-fourth of married women worship without their husbands.

- Less than 10 percent of churches are able to maintain a thriving men's ministry.

- About 90 percent of the boys raised in church abandon it during their teens and 20s never to return.[5]

In a Men in Balance™ survey of churchgoing males, only 50% say their family sees them as a strong spiritual leader.[6] So, who is?

But here is some good news: When the father attends church, the chance that the entire family will attend is 93%. When a mother attends church without the father, the chances of the rest of the family attending are only about 17%. [7]

This points out a lost opportunity for churches. If men are not engaging in good numbers, not only does the church lose their influence and ideas, it loses the leadership talent these men are using in their careers, not to mention the financial contribution they can make to the church mission. The fact that only 10% of churches have a viable men's ministry is especially troubling. That means that (for all practical purposes) the male half of the congregation is not meaningfully engaged beyond attendance. When male newcomers ask for assignments in many churches, too often they are directed to the finance committee or parking attendant roles. That is a travesty. Just think what could happen if all that talent were efficiently channeled into the church mission!

I'm not just complaining about what churches are doing—I'm also making the point that men need to inject themselves into the dialogue and activities, pinpointing needs in the church community and developing solutions—a skill they have in spades! This has tremendous potential for the growth of the church but more importantly, potential for reduced problems with teens, especially boys, when both parents are actively living their values in front of their kids and discussing those values routinely.

My message to men: Your church or synagogue or mosque desperately needs you and you need it. Your spiritual life will be richer, and your family's cohesiveness will be better. With the multitude of places of worship available in most areas, there is almost certainly one where you will find a meaningful home.

Summary

For whatever reasons, women are outpacing men in several key areas of personal development. Too many men are sitting on the sidelines and missing out on self-development options. Men can re-assert their role in the family, where needed, by learning new collaborative approaches. Developing our own skills and talents as men is rewarding and makes us happier as well as more interesting partners. It's also good for our families. It is especially beneficial to churches to have men more involved.

The Balanced Approach

Developing ourselves, as men, must be an ongoing priority. Our families will benefit just as much as we do.

What Are You Going To Do About Your Self Development?

List below a couple of commitments you are willing to make to further your own self development.

Soul-Searching Questions

- If you believe that developing yourself is good for you and your marriage, what will you commit to do about it?
- What aspects of yourself and your development have you ignored? What change is needed?
- In what areas do you need to engage more at home?
- What outside interest or educational opportunity have you pursued lately or postponed?
- Do you long for the ability to talk knowledgeably about more topics instead of the few you know a lot about?
- For you, what would be the payoff of more focus on self-development?
- What dreams for yourself have you been putting off? What are two or three steps you can take in that direction?
- How might a counselor help with your growth?
- How can you become more involved in your place of worship?

Action Steps Men Can Take

- Make a list of things you have always wanted to do, but failed to initiate. Pick one to tackle.
- Start a discussion with your wife about areas for your own development. Ask her what she thinks you would be good at.
- Decide on an area where your talents can help, and sign up this week.
- Create on your smart phone a list of personal development goals with timetables.
- Read some magazines, watch some educational programs outside your normal pattern.
- Check with your place of worship about ways to serve. Make the time commitment.
- Do this for your family: Get an annual physical without fail.
- Record your commitments on the Personal Action Plan on page 194.

Action Steps Women Can Take

- Note skills or talents in your man and suggest he pursue them further. Collect information to get him started.
- Initiate a discussion about his personal dreams and goals. Gently urge action. Show support.
- Research specific opportunities in which he may be interested. Share suggestions, then stop.
- Don't give him a free pass by making decisions without insisting on his input.
- Suggest getting involved in some meaningful volunteer efforts together.
- Remember any "dreams" he has spoken about in the past. Suggest he pursue them.
- Push for mutual spiritual growth in whatever form makes sense to you.
- If your partner already demonstrates a good model in this area, tell him directly.

Ideas for Self-Development

- Take a course on a new subject
- Volunteer at church
- Chair a committee
- Intensely study a subject of your choice
- Book travel to an unfamiliar place
- Have lunch with someone different from you
- Have an in-depth discussion with a teen about music, politics
- Mentor someone in your profession
- Find a mentor for yourself
- Mentor a teen (other than your children)
- Take/audit a course on a topic of your choice
- Set up a testing session for career, competencies
- Attend a church service of another faith
- Start a blog on a topic you are interested in
- Buy a used musical instrument and learn it
- Buy some art supplies and try to draw, paint
- Invite friends over who are from another country
- Buy a book about art or music appreciation

"Traditionally men have not been encouraged to develop good relationship skills."

Lesson 11
Bonus Lesson on Communication

Since you have read this far, I hope you have decided to improve your relationships and especially communication with your partner. That's a good first step.

This may come as a big surprise to many women, but men really do understand that communication is an issue in the relationship. Traditionally, men have not been encouraged to develop good relationship skills beyond what is required in business and minimally interacting with each other socially. This falls far short of what is needed in marriage, and many of the communication techniques which work in a business environment simply do not work in an intimate relationship.

I don't claim to be an expert in relationship communication; however, I have taught hundreds of courses on communication in general and I have learned a lot about relationship communication in my own relationships, and listening to men in small groups. My comments are based on my experience, including tips and pointers that have come out in marriage seminars provided by Men in Balance™ as well as small group sessions I have led. I will cover some basic assumptions about communication in marriage and you can decide if they ring true in your case.

An over-arching suggestion to get started: *Every* substantive communication with your partner (especially when in conflict) should include an affirmation of who they are and how much you appreciate them. This is a need we all have and is usually more important to us than the issue we are discussing.

You Can Change

The good news for men is that you can make dramatic improvements in your communication with your spouse or partner by applying a few simple techniques -- techniques you probably already know and use in a different way at work or in other environments. The good news for women is that by modifying some of your techniques which work in your relationships with other women you can truly connect with your man in a new and exciting way.

A couple of ideas for openers:

1. A good communicator and close friend of mine, Frank McNair says, "Not everyone was raised in your mama's house!"

   What that means is that in your family of origin, you learned a certain style of communication, healthy or not, and the other members of your family learned it as well. Therefore, communication within that small group was fairly simple if not conflict-free. In other words, everybody played by the same rules—healthy or not. So when you enter a relationship with someone totally foreign to your family (i.e. your partner) it may come as a surprise that techniques you have used all your life no longer work. That doesn't mean your techniques are right and the other person's are wrong or vice versa. It simply means the two of you have different styles of communication and it would be really helpful to get on the same page. Then you can create your own (healthy) style of communication that works in your relationship and family. It is reassuring that even though two people come from very different backgrounds, their marriage can still thrive if they learn to deal with differences.

2. Surprise! Men and women do communicate differently! In order to make any progress in communicating with each other, we have to get away from labeling the other person's communication as inferior or inadequate in some way. (She is too emotional. He is insensitive). The fact is that because of our social conditioning we do communicate differently and that is a good thing--something to be celebrated. It is also true that women want men to communicate more like women and vice versa.

Let me give you an example illustrating the difference: If two women are introduced to each other at a party and they sit down to chat, it's likely that within a very few minutes they will know a lot about each other and their families. They will know historical data, and they will have some insight into the person's likes and dislikes. All of this is happening as both women are seemingly talking over each other. The data exchange is astounding. Both parties are picking up on each other's word choice, tone and body language in addition to the words that are actually spoken.

Consider another scenario in which two men meet at a party. Quickly, the conversation turns to vocation and there is some immediate comparison (and measuring) about each other based on the limited data of what each other does for a living. The next level of communication may be about acquaintances they may have in common or some discussion of what projects or other things they may be working on. There may be little eye contact or perceptible body language. And there is almost *no* personal data or relationship information exchanged.

If you think about it, the difference in the two communication styles makes sense. As noted earlier, women's sense of power for most of history has been based on relationship power. They were able to get things done by utilizing relationships to influence others. That was, in many cases, all they had. On the other hand, men have been socialized to be very competitive. This usually suggests the less you reveal, the better your chances of success. So why would you tell potential enemy things that may be used later to destroy you?

Once men and women understand the different approaches of their gender's typical communication, it is easier to start talking about real and substantive things. In this section, we will examine going beyond our differences and limitations and opening up to each other in genuine intimate (couple) conversation, conversation which makes both partners feel they are on the same team, that they know, understand, and trust each other while still allowing each other to be a unique person.

By the way, I am keenly aware that the caricatures above about men and women and their communication styles are total stereotypes and entirely too simple. But for our purposes here, it may serve as a good starting point for discussion.

Why Our Communication Is Not Working

In analyzing communication, you realize that even simple communication has a lot of moving parts. In typical communication, the words you say only represent about 7% of the total communication. Tone of voice carries about 38% and gestures, body language and the like, account for the remaining 55%.[1] This means that when we are lambasting our partner with unnecessary energy in an argument, we are sending so much data that our intent is unmistakable. If he or she hasn't figured out from our sarcastic words that we are upset, perhaps the rage in our face or the blistering tone of voice will make it obvious. We need to ask ourselves whether this is what we really want. What purpose is being served?

It's pretty much impossible to disguise our anger or displeasure. We can try to keep a poker face and reveal very little, but there is still so much data coming from our tone of voice and other sources that our partner is very aware of our feelings.

Also, while it is true you may not be able to control what is said to you, *you can control how you react to it*. So the old idea of counting to 10 when you are upset is probably a good idea. But it's also a good idea to look inside and figure out whether your partner really intended to slight you in some way or whether your own insecurities are bringing out feelings that have no place in the current discussion. It can be very important to ignore the emotion in what she says (it is the emotion that usually hooks us) and listen instead for the message, paraphrasing it back in a neutral manner until she agrees you got it.

What Was the Question?

The first rule of good communication is the use of questions. Using questions instead of offering opinions provides far more valuable information that will keep us from working with false assumptions.

Suppose you are getting ready to go out with your partner and she says something about what you are wearing which you see as disapproval. While you may sense the sudden rush of adrenaline because of the comment, a more rational approach is to ask a simple question, "Do you think this outfit is inappropriate for this evening or what are you trying to say?" Just the few extra seconds you gain by asking the question gives your brain time to reset and allow for some other possibilities, and it allows your partner to resubmit the earlier comment in a less clumsy manner. What just happened is that one partner said something critical, and the other party took the time to clarify the communication rather than light the fuse to some unhealthy fireworks.

This use of questions is one of the main tools in good communication. Asking questions is invaluable for clarifying what is really going on in an argument (instead of what our emotions may be telling us).[2] By asking questions we grant our partner a reprieve while taking responsibility for a miscommunication that may not belong to us but preserves the relationship.

I'm sure you can recall arguments in which you could have used questions to clarify the issues and perhaps stop the dialogue from going in an unhealthy direction. Questions are an excellent safety valve that most of us fail to use when we are tracing the circuitry of an argument. Instead, we let the emotions take over and re-route the power to places it doesn't belong. The result is that the "circuit board" is shorted out or damaged.

The answer to the question at the top of the section is: the reason our communication is not working is that we fail to

1. build in safety checks to make sure we heard accurately before responding, and

2. give our partner a chance to restate what she said using a better choice of words.

The payoff when we discipline ourselves to do this is simply incredible. It puts the two adults in charge and demonstrates a level of trust with each other each that allows each person the right to make a mistake without real consequences.

Prove this to yourself

Next time your partner says something harsh or sarcastic or hostile, instead of responding with your own forceful statement, respond with a question such as:

"Is there a point you wish to make or are you just venting?"

"I'm hearing a lot of energy around this. What do you need from me with this issue?"

"Do you wish me to conclude there is something I have done wrong and you want me to correct it?"

These phrases may sound harsh or awkward, but they put the responsibility back on the speaker to speak in a more appropriate manner.

Paraphrasing

The second tool we have is critical: paraphrasing what we heard (mirroring). Actually, this is the only way we have of telling someone we heard (accurately) what they said. Using phrases such as the ones below, we alert the person that we are about to summarize what they said, proving we "got it."

- So if I heard you correctly, you said.....
- What I hear is your concern about X that.....
- It sounds like you are saying that......

These phrases are helpful in keeping the conversation neutral, on track and advancing properly. They should be followed by a confirmation question, such as "Is that correct?" This ensures accurate transmittal and receipt.

Note to men: When she says you are not listening to her, saying "I can repeat back everything you said." is not the answer. Paraphrasing along the way ensures you get it—and you get credit for getting it.

We all want deep listening or rather to be heard, which is different. Being heard implies being understood and that is what we are after. It does not imply agreement, merely understanding. It will be hard to arrive at this deep level of listening without a sizeable amount of openness on your part. That means you have to remain neutral and non-judgmental about what you are hearing. And one more thing: If you are listening for a problem to be solved, you'll miss most of the message. But once she feels truly heard she no longer feels the need to "stick by her guns" so genuine progress is possible. If you want extra credit, say something like, "Let me see if I can articulate what you are feeling then you tell me what I am missing."

Telling

The third tool is Telling—injecting your own fact or opinion into the discussion. Too often we start, sometimes forcefully, with this tool and never get around to asking questions or truly hearing the response.

- "The way I see it is......" or "Here's what I think..."
- "The invitation says we should be there at 6pm."
- "The checking statement says we are overdrawn. Looks like you failed to record a check or something."

There is a lot more information about these tools on the web or in my earlier book *(having) Better Conversations* available on Amazon. There is much more detail about making the conversation successful. But you can be sure none of us will ever follow all the steps consistently. Frustration, anger, biases, stubbornness—all these keep us from playing by the rules. But if we can do it even 50% of the time, our conversations will be better and we both can be left intact and feeling positive about the discussion.

MAGIC WORDS: "Honey, I know we're disagreeing about this right now and it is really unpleasant for both of us. I'm sorry. We will get through this because I am committed to hearing you out and working through this problem with you. I love you and this issue should not be keeping us apart." You're welcome.

Notes from this section….

"With women, men tend to look for things they can "fix" which keeps them from being able to simply listen to a woman's concerns or ideas."

LESSONS LEARNED/MAIN IDEAS

- Women are expecting more from men today in marriage and are increasingly the ones to file for divorce when the marriage is not satisfactory.

- Many men feel inadequate to deal with the new expectations placed on them. They are frustrated, possibly even surprised to learn that being a good provider is not nearly enough.

- Males have been culturally conditioned early in life to place little emphasis on relationship development and maintenance.

- Some men, often in their 40s, have lost their zest for life and are disillusioned, feeling isolated and spiritually empty. This is usually called "mid-life crisis."

- Work tends to crowd out most other things in life for many men, leaving little room for other interests and/or self-development.

- Some men have a fatalistic view of their situation because they do not believe they are able to fix the complex problems they are facing in their personal lives.

- Most of us inherited our view of women from our father, and our father likely did the same. So our view of women may be out-of-date by two generations.

- Many men withhold their feelings from their partner because they feel she needs protection, or she cannot handle the feelings, or because they want to avoid the conflict that may arise if they make their feelings known.

- When he feels like a failure in his relationship with his partner, a man might resort to drug or alcohol abuse, use of pornography, or womanizing.

- Failing to treat women appropriately can be a real problem in the workplace and can sometimes cost a man his job or marriage or both.

- By the age of seven, boys have begun a trend of paying less attention to relationships and less interaction with girls.

- Anger seems to be the main male emotion acceptable in our

culture. Therefore, it gets overused and other emotions are less developed.

- Men may be less equipped than women to negotiate workable, peaceable solutions to issues. The cultural expectation that they appear strong may be a factor.

- In relationships with women, men tend to look for things they can "fix" which keeps them from being able to passively and empathically listen to a woman's concerns or ideas.

- Lack of proficiency in relationship building and maintenance can make life difficult for men on the job and at home.

- The model of masculinity that we subscribe to is likely to get passed down to our sons.

- Men are more likely than women to resist counseling or seek other support.

- Because men shy away from opening up and sharing with other men, they typically have few close male relationships to provide support when they need it.

- Being stuck in an out-of-date view of masculinity can keep us from being our best selves in relationships or careers.

- Many men consider themselves to be inadequate in a conversation with their partner because they feel their spouse is more articulate.

- Sometimes our preoccupation with acquiring "stuff" and fascination with toys can create distance in relationships as well as skewed priorities.

- Men may feel spiritually empty because they have ignored opportunities to help others or "get outside themselves" in other ways.

- Men and women typically have very different views of intimacy. This can create distance between them and confusion about roles.

- Relationships can be very successful even if there are major differences.

- Erectile dysfunction drugs may fail to work if there are overriding relationship problems.

- Our definition of manliness and masculinity can prevent us from having truly intimate connection with our partner and children.

- Women seem to be paying more attention to self-development than men. For the first time in history, more women than men are graduating from college.

- As men, we tend to become overly focused on work and career at the expense of family and relationships. A third of men consider themselves workaholics, based on the Men in Balance™ survey.

- Sometimes as men we value independence at the expense of close relationships. This can leave us feeling isolated and alone.

- As men, we may have difficulty hearing and acting on feedback, especially from our partner. Failing to factor in our partner's concerns can create problems in a marriage or intimate relationship.

- As men, we are usually taught to be competitors at an early age. For the most part, this works well in sports and career but can be a disaster in personal relationships.

- Unless there are problems at work, most men have probably never studied their communication style so their partner's feedback on the topic may come as a surprise.

- Churches can benefit from committed male involvement in truly significant roles. Men need to take the initiative in asserting themselves into their place of worship.

- There are some well-established rules about interpersonal communication that we can learn to reduce conflict in marriage.

Lessons You Will Use

What are the main things you have learned from this book? Jot them down below. If there are life lessons you have learned elsewhere, include those as well.

"Many men believe they can solve their own problems and don't need outside help."

Other Lessons

Here are a few other lessons men have shared with me. Perhaps they will be useful to you.

Don't get involved in an affair

In today's culture, having an affair is sort of like an achievement badge. Certainly, the popular music and culture seem to glorify it. But it is fraught with problems. If you are tempted to have an affair because of problems in your marriage, first seek help to solve the problems, keeping in mind that half of those problems are likely on your side of the ledger. If you're not willing to go to counseling, then leave the marriage rather than risk damaging yourself, your wife and family, and possibly your career.

Don't resist counseling

I've talked to a lot of men whose wives made valiant efforts to get them into counseling to resolve marital issues. Many men believe they can solve their own problems and don't need outside help. This can be a deal breaker for the marriage. If you are willing to have your car worked on when it is acting strangely or you believe in routine maintenance for your home, why not for your marriage as well? So much more is at stake and it is the healthy, manly thing to do. If you're unhappy in your marriage, it may be hard for you to believe that the two of you can be wildly crazy about each other again, but counseling can help get you there. See page 203 for options.

Attend to your spiritual side

Whether you consider yourself to be religious or not, you do have a spiritual side and it needs nurturing. Decide what that means for you and pursue it. The alternative is to ignore that side of you until there is a crisis, or until your life seems so empty you pursue unhealthy activities such as having an affair or involving yourself in pornography or worse. Get some books on the subject or talk to a minister or counselor and learn more about your spiritual self. Drug and alcohol addiction have been labeled universally as symptoms of a spiritual deficit.

Get rid of bad habits

Take a good hard look at your life and decide what needs to be changed. Are you drinking too much? Are you flirting with women in the office which could jeopardize your job and marriage? Have you considered morally questionable business deals? Is your work life so out of balance that the family seems to be operating without you?

Are you involved in pornography that could lead to some embarrassing incidents? In our survey 31% of men admitted to having a dark side which they would not want others to know about.[1]

Many men have confided in me that in some ways they feel they are an imposter, a fraud, living a role instead of being the authentic man we talked about earlier in the chapter on masculinity. They wonder if the best they can provide is truly enough. Sometimes the tremendous responsibilities we carry, the need to conform to keep our job or other pressures known only to men can cause us to forget who we really are and what our true values represent. Those pressures can also lead us astray.

Do you remember John Edwards? A Vice-Presidential candidate, his story reminds us how easy it is to have a "private self" that is different from the public one we present to everyone else. What makes this particularly sad is that Edwards was taking contributions from people while representing himself as something he was not--a trustworthy, morally upright, and honest person. Worse, he was talking about the need for strong moral convictions for Americans. Now his political career is over and his image is soiled forever.

A man I know went to prison because of a "private life" that only he and a few others knew about. He can never recover the damage done to his family and his career, but he is now coaching others facing prison as a way of seeking some redemption.

Many of us can somehow "segment" or compartmentalize our lives and find ways to justify (we think) living one way while proclaiming to be something else. For example, some men are church leaders but are hooked on pornography or are involved in affairs.

Nurture the kids

If you are not actively involved in raising and nurturing your children, remedy that. Parenting is a two-person job and not something you can delegate to your partner. The involvement of the father in a child's life is a good predictor of how that child will turn out. There is no substitute for the guidance of a strong spiritually healthy man in a child's life. Don't slight your daughters in handing out guidance and direction.

Steer clear of anything that smells questionable

Every week news stories report men who have become involved in questionable financial dealings, exploitation of clients, attempting to circumvent a law, or other questionable behavior. You have worked hard to build your career and it would be a travesty to have that explode in your face. No matter how careful you may be and how much you think this cannot happen to you, there are men serving time in prison who would tell you otherwise. A good test is this: If your behavior became the subject for discussion on the front page of the paper tomorrow, how would that make you feel?

Cherish your partner

Widowers tell me they wish they had another opportunity to say kind words and be a strong support for their partners. You've heard it before: Life is not a dress rehearsal for something else. It is the real thing. Tomorrow is not guaranteed to anyone, so show your affection and love for your partner today. Pamper her in ways that make her know she is truly important in your life. She needs to feel cherished just like you need to feel valued and respected. In our survey, 46% of men acknowledged that they sometimes do not treat their wives well.[2]

Admit your mistakes

The 4th step in the Alcoholics Anonymous twelve-step program requires you to do a thorough moral inventory (see **Resources**). There is good reason for this. If you have failings in your personal life, it is important to root out the causes for those, deal with them and make amends. Be honest about behaviors that have caused problems in your life and potentially threaten to derail your marriage or career. If they are psychological issues, get help from a counselor. If it involves questionable or morally questionable activity, talk with your minister or other trusted advisor. Peace comes by acknowledging your humanity, admitting you are not perfect, and realizing that people who love you accept you in spite of your flaws.

Add a little humility

It is great that we all have a certain amount of ego. It serves us well when we need a dose of courage or feel inadequate. But an overinflated ego can cause you to be callous to other people. It can also convince you that you are invincible, or get you involved in things that are not healthy. Our culture rewards people who walk with a swagger, have all the right answers and talk tough. Indeed, that model works well in some business settings. But my experience is that it doesn't work forever. Showing a little humility and willingness to be influenced is a valuable trait in a marriage or a career. The best leaders as judged by their followers are those who listen to others along the way and make every effort to bring others along. There are numerous books on this topic if you want to pursue the subject. The point is not to allow your own ego to drive your behaviors and decisions.

Have a strong moral compass

Every day we are called on to make decisions, large and small, which can benefit us and/or hurt others. Those decisions might range from an executive order to change the parking arrangements in a way that favors executives, to helping someone asking for money on a street corner. Life tends to harden us into thinking that people should be able to take care of themselves, but it is worth noting that throughout history, caring for others, especially the poor, has been a major tenet of most successful civilizations and is a central tenet of Jesus's teaching. If you are not involved in charitable causes, if you are not donating regularly to organizations committed to helping others, if you are not speaking out against legislation that disadvantages those who have no voice, do something about that. Not only is it a manly thing to do, it is the *right* thing to do.

Become less judgmental

Making judgments about people based on our own biases and prejudices is so easy—and deadly. Being judgmental causes us to stereotype entire groups of people, blame others for problems in our lives, and narrows our viewpoint of what is acceptable. It robs us of rewarding relationships with people who are different from us. Cable TV and talk radio encourage us to disagree forcefully with one group or another. There are few voices asking us to learn to appreciate differences, value diverse thinking and give up trying to change others. Take a few moments daily to challenge your own thinking, asking yourself what you may be missing by making quick judgments about people or ideas.

"At a minimum, we can let this be our motto, 'If this marriage fails, it won't be because I gave up on it or did not give it my all.'"

GOING FORWARD

What is the Ideal Man?

Comedian and former priest Mark Gungor asked women what they want in a man. When they listed all the qualities they would like, he says, "That's another woman!"[1]

To many men, that may seem sadly true. The qualities we have been trained to exhibit can seem suddenly archaic and out of place. Not what the women are looking for. That doesn't mean we are out of the relationship game, but it likely means there will be more and more of us trying to sort out roles and needs in a complex relationship, made more so with the crushing demands of career and raising children.

If a woman feels that her emotional needs are not being met, she is not getting adequate help with household duties and child rearing, or her husband is absorbed in work or personal interests, she might reasonably ask, "What's the point? I can manage just as well alone."

This is a clarion call to men: Hear, truly hear, your partner's frustrations. Open up and share yours in a healthy way. Put aside ego and defensiveness and join your partner in this daunting task we call marriage. Surely marriage has its challenges, but it also has tremendous rewards for those willing to work at it. And working at it might mean some (or a lot of) counseling, flexibility of roles, willingness to share feelings, giving up stereotypical ideas about "what marriage should be" and a willingness to deal with what your marriage is. At a minimum, we can let this be our motto, "If this marriage fails, it won't be because I gave up on it or did not give it my all."

Good luck.

"There is help for your situation."

Resources and Things to Think About

On the following pages are additional items to add to the mix as you think about your own program of self-improvement.

Resource: Quiz--Is your life in balance?

Take this short quiz. Feel free to share with others. Give yourself 5 points for each TRUE answer. A score of 70 or less might mean you should take some action.

1. I am satisfied with the number of hours I work each week.
2. Work is NOT an issue between my spouse/partner and me.
3. I have close MALE friends with whom I can truly share everything about myself.
4. I have a tension-free sex life with my spouse/partner.
5. I enjoy sex and rarely, if ever, have difficulty in this area.
6. I have a close relationship with my children (if applicable).
7. I almost never miss family activities and I am *fully present* when participating.
8. I have never had an affair or cheated on my partner.
9. I am satisfied with my career and the demands it makes on me.
10. I enjoy my work and feel I am making a significant contribution.
11. I have a strong faith relationship.
12. I pray regularly (at least weekly).
13. I am involved in at least one organization that helps others.
14. I attend church/worship regularly.
15. I am satisfied with the communication between my wife/partner and me.
16. I am satisfied with the communication between my children and me (if applicable).
17. I have never lost a friendship over anger or failing to respect the other person.

(Continued...)

18. I have a good financial plan which should support me in retirement OR
    I have a good financial plan which will educate my children.
19. I do not have a problem with drugs (including alcohol), pornography, or womanizing.
20. I have no serious "dark side" that I would never want exposed.
21. I have friends who trust me to listen without judgment when they are having problems.
22. I am comfortable talking with other men about my personal life and beliefs.
23. I have made serious attempts to work on my own "issues" through counseling or self-study.

___ My score

Resource: (AT LEAST) 10 MISTAKES GUYS MAKE IN COMMUNICATING WITH WOMEN

1. Fixing (or attempting to fix) instead of empathizing.

    (Try saying: "I'm sorry that happened to you."

    "That must be very frustrating. How can I help?")

2. Focusing on the facts/details instead of the relationship.

    (Instead of saying "You can change your schedule easier than I can," try "It sounds like you need me to re-schedule that meeting so I can go with you to the church dinner. I understand that is really important to you.")

3. Making the decision, then communicating it (instead of getting her input and making the decision together).

    ("I've decided we can buy the boat and remodel the kitchen later.")

4. Interrupting instead of paraphrasing back her concern (reloading your guns).

5. Sarcasm.

    ("Yeah, well your parents sometimes don't even know I'm in the family.")

6. One upsmanship or "Yes, but…"

("Oh, you think you are stressed, let me tell you about my day.")

7. Telling her what she thinks or feels

   ("You think you can just do whatever you want and get away with it. You just don't care.")

8. Making "you" statements instead of "I" statements. Sounds like blaming.

   ("You embarrass me when you do something like that." vs. "When you do that, I feel embarrassed.")

   Turn it from a complaint into a request: "Look, I would really appreciate it if you wouldn't talk about that incident with our friends."

9. Generalizing from this problem to something universal.

   ("See, being late for this just shows how little you care about what's important to me.")

10. Absolutes/Superlatives.

    ("You *always* forget to lock the door." "*Everything* you said was hostile toward my friends.")

11. (BONUS) Defensiveness.

> ("Yes, I overspent but it was because you didn't balance the checkbook accurately. You're always making errors and then I get in trouble.")

Special note: The biggest mistake we make is avoiding the conversation and withdrawing instead of dealing with the conflict in a healthy way! Most counselors will tell you avoiding conflict is a recipe for trouble.

Resource: 20 Assumptions About Marriage

from Men in Balance™ www.meninbalance.org

1) Conflict is inevitable so trying to avoid it is futile. Learning to manage it is imperative.
2) Men and women have fundamentally different ways of viewing the same information which can cause unexpected communication problems in a marriage.
3) Most of our ideas about what constitutes a "healthy" marriage are formed in our family of origin and will probably not match those of our spouse.
4) Our individual ego and pride can be major obstacles to a healthy marriage.
5) Speaking up for our own needs in a marriage is not only healthy, it is essential.
6) The demands and stress of maintaining a family can and likely will create distance between spouses. A conscious effort to reduce that distance is critical to a healthy marriage.
7) Differences in sexual appetites between spouses is normal but needs to be negotiated in a mutually agreeable manner.
8) Most marriages will at some point need counseling from an outside source. Both parties must be willing to participate and be willing to change for the sake of the marriage.
9) Too much attention to career(s) or other distractions can cause couples to drift apart.
10) Healthy marriages require intentional effort and routine maintenance.

11) Romantic love may be the beginning foundation of a relationship, but will not sustain a marriage over time. The definition of love must change as the marriage matures.

12) There is no "formula" for what constitutes a good marriage. A "good" marriage is determined by the individuals and what works practically for them.

13) Communication is one of the most troublesome hurdles in most relationships, and certainly is in marriage. Good communication is a skill which can be learned.

14) Blended families and mixed marriages have unique problems which will get worse if not dealt with.

15) Open dialogue is essential to a truly healthy marriage and this requires that both parties be open and transparent in their discussions. This may be more difficult for men in some cases, but it is a skill that can be learned.

16) Money, sex, children, discipline, career, religion and family are among the most troublesome issues for most marriages. You may need help with these.

17) Second and third marriages tend to have even lower success rates than first marriages, indicating that we don't learn from our mistakes.

18) Wounds we carry from childhood and which we may not even be aware of can cause problems in any relationship but are almost guaranteed to cause problems in marriage because of its demand for intimacy and closeness.

19) Children can become accomplished manipulators of parents. It is extremely important that both parents be "on the same page" regarding discipline and family expectations.

20) Absolute and unconditional trust between partners may be an impossible ideal, but must be constantly the goal.

Resource: Couples Communication Guidelines

from Men in Balance™ www.meninbalance.org

- Most important decision (made each day): We will stay together.
- Unresolved conflict creates distance in the relationship.
- Successfully resolving issues builds trust, intimacy. It shows your relationship is strong enough to withstand challenges. Avoiding issues means you are not sure.
- Finding your "higher calling" in your marriage puts smaller issues in perspective.
- Intimacy is being able to reveal your true self knowing that it will not be used against you later.
- We must allow each other momentary frustrations without making a big issue of it or taking it personally.
- We can be the "container" for our partner's anger or frustration, allowing them to vent.
- Emotions are fleeting--sometimes it is best to let them pass without responding (especially when they are coming from our partner).
- It is important to speak up for what we want and represent ourselves truthfully in the relationship.
- We need to be clear about our boundaries and expect our partner to respect them.

- Defensiveness can be destructive and shuts down further dialogue.
- The only way to work on our own issues is IN a relationship.
- Assuming positive intent on the part of your partner can keep you from attributing sinister motives.
- Our partner is not our parent, our ex, our former lover--so we should not read into their actions our own assumptions or weaknesses.
- The best gift we can give each other is a healthy, loving relationship.
- Tone of voice and body language matter at least as much in partner communication as the words you say.

Resource: A special note about fathers and their influence...

For good reason, the first session of most Men in Balance™ programs is about fathers and their influence. When I ask groups of men, large and small, how many of them had a good relationship with their fathers, only a few hands go up. When I ask how many had a troublesome relationship with their father, many hands go up. This has been consistent since I started the organization in 2007.

What are the implications of this? It means that one of the most important relationships in our life is either missing or troubled. If you are one of the few men who have a good relationship with your father and are pleased with that relationship, you are truly blessed. For many more of us, the father was either absent or highly critical or damaging in his approach to raising us.

There is a tremendous irony here: We adored our fathers in most cases and emulated their behavior in virtually every way possible. However, as adults, we find that their thinking may have been flawed or their attitudes not useful by today's standards. The way they modeled their involvement in the household, treatment of their wife, treatment of their children – – all of these were largely appropriated into our behaviors as well. In many cases that model has not served us well and has created problems for a whole new generation.

Men who have suffered verbal abuse at the hands of their father (possibly as simple as put downs about their masculinity or worthiness) face special challenges. Those who suffered physical/sexual abuse (and that number is larger than you might think) deserve our sincere empathy and support. Those scars are permanent and literally inform almost every facet of our lives, especially close relationships. (How could you ever trust anyone again?) If you are in that group, please begin to find a way out of your suffering through counseling or other help. It is key to remember you did nothing to warrant the abuse.

In my opinion, it is time to stop the madness. My hope for men is that they realize they are not obligated to follow their father's model. They are not obligated to do things his way or attempt to gain his support or approval. As an adult male, we have the right and the privilege to be our own person and to manage our personal lives and raise our children as we see fit. That means adopting a different way of treating wives and children. It may also suggest a different way of expressing emotion, acceptance and vulnerability.

The 21st Century Man

As this book has illustrated, women are looking for a different type of man in the 21st century. They rightfully expect a man to be an emotional support and soul mate who can be tender when needed and tough when required. It is no longer acceptable for us to isolate ourselves in an emotional vacuum chamber and not engage on a human level. It is not only okay, it is a good thing to:

- be open and vulnerable with your partner
- be loving and supportive of your children
- provide spiritual guidance for your family
- show tenderness and emotion easily
- cry publicly when emotions call for that
- seek out counsel when your marriage is in trouble
- teach your children to respect all people
- actively engage in child play with your children
- consistently help your partner with household chores
- own up to your failures

- use good communication techniques that invite collaboration
- assume positive intent on the part of your partner

It may be hard for us to realize that our fathers could have led us astray with their beliefs. We can be sympathetic to the fact that they probably inherited those ideas from their fathers and we have no way of knowing whether those ideas worked unless we saw open warfare between our parents.

A New Kind of Father

I believe what is called for now is a new kind of father who acknowledges his essential role in the family as a life partner and as a powerful co-leader with his partner for his children. Even if you are divorced, your goal should be to stay very active in your children's life. You should insist on as much time with your children as possible and make sure you are giving them the best counsel you can, counsel that is grounded in strong moral and spiritual roots and will serve them as adults for the rest of their life. You do not have the right to abandon this responsibility.

If you are a new father, study how to be a good parent. Disregard any questionable advice from your own father and seek out opportunities to learn about your important role. If you are a stepparent, your role as a central male figure is very important. Clarify with your partner areas like discipline and direction, but don't hold back from presenting a healthy, strong male role model for stepchildren of any age.

Finally, if you have not already done so, make peace with your own father about any outstanding issues. Trust me. If he dies without your having done this, it will trouble you for days to come. In one of our sessions, a man talked about his troubled relationship with his father and how it consumed much of his adult life. As he began his second marriage, his father developed a terminal illness which required him to move in with his son. This man became so angry that his father was intruding yet again, he shook his fist at the heavens in anger – – so much that he threw his back out and had to begin bed rest himself. In the same room with his father. Although there were fireworks at first, he said "I finally got to know the old man." He teared up as he told the story realizing the lost years he and his father had spent estranged from each other. Life has a way, does it not?

I would love to hear your stories about your relationship with your father and any lessons you have learned over the years. My email is: jerry@meninbalance.org.

Resource: Men in Balance Survey Results

Here are the results of the survey. This is not a scientific survey — it is biased in favor of church-going men, our target audience (note the percent saying they regularly attend church).

	% answering agree or strongly agree
Work	
I tend to work more hours than my job requires.	52%
I work more than 40 hours a week because my job requires it.	54%
I am able to control my work hours and generally work 40 hours a week or less.	37%
My work causes me to miss family events.	34%
I get a great deal of satisfaction from my work even though it requires long hours.	62%
The primary reason I work hard is to maintain or improve our standard of living.	68%
I feel a great deal of pressure to provide well for my family.	70%
I have a strong sense of identity with my job.	71%
I have had conflicts with my spouse over the number of hours I work.	34%
I sometimes bring the frustrations of work home with me.	68%
I am able to forget about work once I am home with my family.	48%

My partner understands the work commitments required of me and is supportive.	71%
I would rather work fewer hours and make less money.	25%
I sometimes get so absorbed in my work I forget about the time.	63%
I have received promotions which required a substantially larger amount of my time.	39%
I am able to go on vacation or weekend trips and forget about work.	64%
I tend to check my voicemail or email when I am with my family.	64%
I am aware that work takes time away from my family but I don't feel I have a choice.	50%
I have turned down promotions in order to have more time with my family.	24%
If I am honest with myself, I am a workaholic.	33%
My work and personal life are in balance, more or less.	62%
I have no real hobbies which occupy my time.	33%
I feel a lot of pressure to increase my family's standard of living.	52%
I have no one I can really talk to about work demands.	36%
I miss being able to take more time with my family.	51%
Frequently I am too tired to really enjoy downtime or family time.	48%

Connection

I have no close male friends with whom I can talk openly about personal issues.	46%

I sometimes feel isolated about my personal life.	65%
I can talk openly with my partner about almost everything.	68%
My partner understands me and is supportive.	79%
I would like to be in a small group of men with whom I could share my thoughts and feelings.	62%
I would like to be more able to open up and talk with other men about personal issues.	67%
Most people would probably say I am a "private" person and do not talk much about personal issues.	61%
I have 5 or more "good friends" with whom I can be myself.	51%

Communication

My partner and I communicate well with few problems.	60%
My partner would like me to talk more.	61%
I do not enjoy talking to my partner about our relationship.	36%
I have concerns about my marriage/relationship I have not shared with my partner.	39%
I can sense when my partner has a concern and invite a discussion.	73%
There are a number of issues my partner and I simply cannot discuss.	37%
My partner does not understand the many pressures I am under.	43%
I enjoy "quiet communion time" with my partner.	70%

My partner and I talk at least a few minutes each day about things other than "logistics and schedules".	72%
I do not have problems communicating at work, but I do at home.	32%
I am difficult to communicate with at home.	30%
I sometimes do not treat my partner very well.	46%
I tend to avoid conflict in close relationships.	63%
My partner and I can discuss differences calmly and come to agreement.	63%
My partner and I are in agreement about most family issues.	75%

Personal Intimacy

My partner and I have a rewarding, close relationship.	68%
I wish my partner were more supportive of me.	35%
I have a satisfying sex life with my partner.	51%
I consider my partner to also be a best friend with whom I can talk freely.	77%
I have lost the enthusiasm for my relationship with my partner.	26%
I would like to be able to open up more with my partner.	56%
My partner has suggested counseling but I have resisted.	6%
I enjoy sex and rarely, if ever, have difficulty in this area.	62%
I have never had an affair or cheated on my partner.	78%
I would like more conversation with my partner.	66%

I don't feel I know how to have a productive conversation with my partner on sensitive issues.	42%
I sometimes am critical of my partner around others.	24%
I would like more sex from my partner.	63%
I almost never miss family activities and I am **fully present** when participating.	74%

Family life

Our family typically has at least one meal together.	74%
My children openly share their feelings and concerns.	63%
I can be a "best friend" to my children and listen without offering advice or judgment.	60%
Our family frequently does things together (other than meals).	79%
I am disappointed in the amount of together time in my family.	42%
My children would say I am very involved in their lives.	66%
My children are involved in church activities other than worship.	49%
I make sure my children are in church almost every week.	48%
Our family has regular devotions or prayer.	37%
I am viewed by my family as a strong spiritual leader.	50%
My children enjoy family time together.	79%
My partner and I are in agreement about issues involving children including discipline.	63%
I wish I could communicate better with my children.	52%

My children would say I criticize them a lot.	20%
My family members talk openly about issues that are bothering them.	62%

Spiritual

My spiritual life is satisfying.	66%
I have a strong faith relationship with God.	78%
I pray regularly (at least weekly).	82%
I am involved in at least one organization that helps others.	76%
I attend church/worship regularly.	74%
I am actively involved in some church activity other than attending worship.	65%
I usually make time for regular church attendance.	74%

Personal

I do not have a problem with drugs (including alcohol), pornography, or womanizing.	75%
I have no serious "dark side" that I would never want exposed.	69%
I have friends who trust me to listen without judgment when they are having problems.	84%
I am comfortable talking with other men about my personal life, beliefs.	73%
I have made serious attempts to work on my own "issues" through counseling or self-study.	82%
I believe men should be able to handle problems on their own without resorting to counseling or coaching.	25%

I feel I have some unfinished business with my father (living or dead).	44%
My father provided an excellent role model for my life.	56%
My father was absent (emotionally or physically) or critical of me.	54%
I take good care of my health and have regular check-ups.	84%

Resource: The Twelve Steps of Alcoholics Anonymous

(Provided as a methodology to solve other problems in your life)

1. We admitted we were powerless over alcohol - that our lives had become unmanageable.

2. Came to believe that a Power greater than ourselves could restore us to sanity.

3. Made a decision to turn our will and our lives over to the care of God as we understood Him.

4. Made a searching and fearless moral inventory of ourselves.

5. Admitted to God, to ourselves and to another human being the exact nature of our wrongs.

6. Were entirely ready to have God remove all these defects of character.

7. Humbly asked Him to remove our shortcomings.

8. Made a list of all persons we had harmed, and became willing to make amends to them all.

9. Made direct amends to such people wherever possible, except when to do so would injure them or others.

10. Continued to take personal inventory and when we were wrong promptly admitted it.

11. Sought through prayer and meditation to improve our conscious contact with God as we understood Him, praying only for knowledge of His will for us and the power to carry that out.

12. Having had a spiritual awakening as the result of these steps, we tried to carry this message to alcoholics and to practice these principles in all our affairs.

Resources: Books and Videos

Books

Amen, Daniel G. *Change Your Brain, Change Your Life: The Breakthrough Program for Conquering Anxiety, Depression, Obsessiveness, Anger, and Impulsiveness*. New York: Times, 2000. Print.

Boyd, Stephen Blake. *The Men We Long to Be: Beyond Domination to a New Christian Understanding of Manhood*. San Francisco: Harper San Francisco, 1995. Print.

Bly, Robert. *Iron John: A Book about Men*. Reading, MA: Addison-Wesley, 1990. Print.

Chapman, Gary D. *The Five Love Languages: How to Express Heartfelt Commitment to Your Mate*. Chicago: Northfield Pub., 2004. Print.

Eldredge, John. *Wild at Heart: Discovering the Passionate Soul of a Man*. Nashville, TN: T. Nelson, 2001. Print.

Eldredge, John. *Wild at Heart: Discovering the Secret of a Man's Soul*. Nashville, TN: Thomas Nelson, 2001. Print.

Farrell, Warren. *Why Men Are the Way They Are: The Male-female Dynamic*. New York: McGraw-Hill, 1986. Print.

Friedman, Martin G. *Straight Talk for Men about Marriage: What Men Need to Know about Marriage (and What Women Need to Know about Men)*. Beverly Hills, CA: Little Moose, 2005. Print.

Gottman, John Mordechai., and Nan Silver. *The Seven Principles for Making Marriage Work*. New York: Three Rivers, 1999. Print.

Hendrix, Harville. *Getting the Love You Want: A Guide for Couples*. New York: H. Holt, 2008. Print.

Keen, Sam. *Fire in the Belly: On Being a Man*. New York: Bantam, 1991. Print.

Love, Patricia. How to Improve Your Marriage Without Talking About It. Broadway Press, 2007. Print

Morley, Patrick M. *The Man in the Mirror: Solving the 24 Problems Men Face*. Brentwood, TN: Wolgemuth & Hyatt, 1989. Print.

Murrow, David. *Why Men Hate Going to Church*. Nashville: Nelson, 2005. Print.

Rohr, Richard. *Quest for the Grail.* New York: Crossroad, 1994. Print.

Struthers, William M. *Wired for Intimacy: How Pornography Hijacks the Brain*, 2010, IVP Books

Tannen, Deborah. *You Just Don't Understand: Women and Men in Conversation*. New York, NY: Morrow, 1990. Print.

Websites:

10lessonsformen.com
meninbalance.org
goodtherapy.org
beckinstitute.org (CBT)
Joshua Project

Video/DVD
Cognitive Behavioral Therapy: Techniques for Retraining Your Brain, Course No. 9631 Great Courses, Professor Jason M. Satterfield, Ph.D.

Article

The Neuroscience of Leadership. David Rock and Jeffrey Schwartz www.strategy-business.com.

My Personal Action Plan

These are the things I plan to work on...

BIBLIOGRAPHY

Introduction

1. Wang, Yanan. "Women Are More Likely to Initiate Divorce." *The Washington Post*. WP Company, 27 Aug. 2015. Web. 23 July 2017. <https://www.washingtonpost.com/news/soloish/wp/2015/08/27/why-women-are-more-likely-to-initiate-divorce/?utm_term=.e0057390ec3a>.

Lesson One: Broadening Our Narrow View of Masculinity

1. Real, Terrence. "Chapter One: Are You Getting What You Want?" *The New Rules of Marriage: What You Need to Know to Make Love Work*. New York: Ballantine, 2008. N. pag. Print.

2. "The Weaker Sex." *The Economist*. The Economist Newspaper, 30 May 2015. Web. 20 July 2017. <https://www.economist.com/news/leaders/21652323-blue-collar-men-rich-countries-are-trouble-they-must-learn-adapt-weaker-sex>.

Lesson Two: Improving Our Attitude Toward Women

1. Friedman, Martin G. "Chapter Two." *Straight Talk for Men about Marriage: What Men Need to Know about Marriage (and What Women Need to Know about Men)*. Beverly Hills, CA: Little Moose, 2005. N. pag. Print.

2. Tran, Robin. "4 Ways Men Are Taught to Objectify Women From Birth." *Everyday Feminism*. N.p., 20 June 2016. Web. 23 July 2017. <http://everydayfeminism.com/2016/06/men-taught-to-objectify-women/>.

3. Real, Terrence. "Small Murders: How We Lose Passion." *How Can I Get through to You?: Closing the Intimacy Gap between Men and Women*. New York: Scribner, 2002. N. pag. Print.

4. Lang, Gregory. *Why a Daughter Needs a Dad*. N.p.: Cumberland House, 2017. Print.

5. Chira, Susan. "The Universal Phenomenon of Men Interrupting Women." *New York Times*. N.p., 14 June 2017. Web. 20 July 2017. <https://www.nytimes.com/2017/06/14/business/women-sexism-work-huffington-kamala-harris.html?mc=aud_dev&mcid=fb-nytimes&mccr=July48Fem&mcdt=2017-07&subid=July48Fem&ad-keywords=AudDevGate&_r=0>.

Lesson Three: Removing Our Fear of Real Intimacy

1. Hancock, Jerry T. "Men in Balance Survey Results." *Survey Results*. Men in Balance, n.d. Web. 21 July 2017. <http://meninbalance.org/index.php/see-survey-results>.

2. "Therapy for Men's Issues and Problems." *GoodTherapy.org*. N.p., n.d. Web. 20 July 2017. <http://www.goodtherapy.org/learn-about-therapy/issues/men-issues>.

3. Gottman, John Mordechai., PH.D., and Nan Silver. "Chapter Seven: The Two Kinds of Marital Conflict." *The Seven Principles for Making Marriage Work*. New York: Three Rivers, 2000. N. pag. Print.

4. Love, Patricia. How to Improve Your Marriage Without Talking About It. Broadway Press, 2007. Print

5. Hancock, Jerry T. "Men in Balance Survey Results." *Survey Results*. Men in Balance, n.d. Web. 21 July 2017. <http://meninbalance.org/index.php/see-survey-results>.

Lesson Four: Working on Our Relationship Skills

1. Gottman, John Mordechai, and Nan Silver. "Chapter Six: Let Your Partner Influence You." *The Seven Principles for Making Marriage Work*. New York: Harmony, 2015. N. pag. Print.

2. Hancock, Jerry T. "Men in Balance Survey Results." *Survey Results*. Men in Balance, n.d. Web. 21 July 2017. <http://meninbalance.org/index.php/see-survey-results>.

3. Gottman, John Mordechai, and Nan Silver. "Chapter Ten: Overcome Gridlock." *The Seven Principles for Making Marriage Work*. New York: Harmony, 2015. N. pag. Print.

4. Hancock, Jerry T. "Men in Balance Survey Results." *Survey Results*. Men in Balance, n.d. Web. 21 July 2017. <http://meninbalance.org/index.php/see-survey-results>.

5. Hancock, Jerry T. "Men in Balance Survey Results." *Survey Results*. Men in Balance, n.d. Web. 21 July 2017. <http://meninbalance.org/index.php/see-survey-results>.

Lesson Five: Why Our Focus on Competition Is Incompatible with Relationships

1. Highfield, Roger. "Study Finds Women Cooperate Better than Men." *The Telegraph*. Telegraph Media Group, 26 Sept. 2007. Web. 21 July 2017. <http://www.telegraph.co.uk/news/science/science-news/3308347/Study-finds-women-cooperate-better-than-men.html>.

2. *Learn | 2020 Women on Boards*. N.p., 10 Dec. 2011. Web. 21 July 2017. <https://www.2020wob.com/learn>.

3. Weaver, Richard G., and John D. Farrell. *Managers as Facilitators: A Practical Guide to Getting Work Done in a Changing Workplace*. San Francisco: Berrett-Koehler, 1999. Print.

Lesson Six: Why Our Focus on Career Robs us of Connection

1. Hancock, Jerry T. "Men in Balance Survey Results." *Survey Results*. Men in Balance, n.d. Web. 21 July 2017. <http://meninbalance.org/index.php/see-survey-results>.

2. Hancock, Jerry T. "Men in Balance Survey Results." *Survey Results*. Men in Balance, n.d. Web. 21 July 2017. <http://meninbalance.org/index.php/see-survey-results>.

3. Weissmann, Jordan. "Is There Really Such a Thing as a 'Workaholic'?" *The Atlantic*. Atlantic Media Company, 19 Feb. 2014. Web. 21 July 2017. <https://www.theatlantic.com/magazine/archive/2013/09/the-work-addiction/309437/>.

4. Morley, Patrick M. *The Man in the Mirror: Solving the 24 Problems Men Face*. Grand Rapids, MI: Zondervan House, 2000. Print.

Lesson Seven: How Our Focus on Independence Makes Us Unapproachable

1. Wood, Wendy. "Five Myths about Our Habits." *The Washington Post*. WP Company, 31 Dec. 2015. Web. 22 July 2017. <https://www.washingtonpost.com/opinions/five-myths-about-our-habits/2015/12/31/1f3ab244-ad93-11e5-9ab0-884d1cc4b33e_story.html?utm_term=.16bd3f185633>.

2. Mayo Clinic Staff. "Cognitive Behavioral Therapy." *Mayo Clinic*. Mayo Foundation for Medical Education and Research, 23 Feb. 2016. Web. 22 July 2017. <http://www.mayoclinic.org/tests-procedures/cognitive-behavioral-therapy/home/ovc-20186868>.

Lesson Eight: How Our Preoccupation with Toys Keeps Us from Connecting

1. Walters, Joanna. "Tablets and Smartphones May Affect Social and Emotional Development, Scientists Speculate." *The Guardian*. Guardian News and Media, 02 Feb. 2015. Web. 22 July 2017. <https://www.theguardian.com/technology/2015/feb/01/toddler-brains-research-smartphones-damage-social-development>.

2. Bob Dylan. "The Times They Are a-Changin'." *The Times They Are a-Changin'*, Columbia Studios, 1964.

Lesson Nine: Our Difficulty Receiving and Learning from Feedback Leaves Us Isolated

1. Lindsay, Nicole. "Taking Constructive Criticism Like a Champ." *The Muse*. N.p., 02 Nov. 2012. Web. 22 July 2017. <https://www.themuse.com/advice/taking-constructive-criticism-like-a-champ>.

2. Hawkins, David. "Why You Should Always Assume Positive Intent." *Crosswalk.com*. Salem Web Network, 16 Aug. 2016. Web. 22 July 2017. <http://www.crosswalk.com/family/marriage/doctor-david/why-you-should-always-assume-positive-intent.html>.

Lesson Ten: How Our Failure to Develop Our Whole Selves Leaves Us Incomplete

1. "The Weaker Sex." *The Economist*. The Economist Newspaper, 30 May 2015. Web. 20 July 2017. <https://www.economist.com/news/leaders/21652323-blue-collar-men-rich-countries-are-trouble-they-must-learn-adapt-weaker-sex>.

2. "The Weaker Sex." *The Economist*. The Economist Newspaper, 30 May 2015. Web. 20 July 2017. <https://www.economist.com/news/leaders/21652323-blue-collar-men-rich-countries-are-trouble-they-must-learn-adapt-weaker-sex>.

3. Gottman, John Mordechai, and Nan Silver. "Chapter Ten: Overcome Gridlock." *The Seven Principles for Making Marriage Work*. New York: Harmony, 2015. N. pag. Print.

4. Murrow, David. "Ministry and the Masculine Spirit." *Why Men Hate Going to Church*. Nashville, TN: Thomas Nelson, 2005. N. pag. Print.

5. "New Study Profiles Women's Use of Health Care." *Centers for Disease Control and Prevention*. Centers for Disease Control and Prevention, 22 Jan. 2010. Web. 22 July 2017.

<https://www.cdc.gov/nchs/pressroom/01news/newstudy.htm>.

6. Murrow, David. "The Gap of Presence." *Why Men Hate Going to Church*. Nashville, TN: Thomas Nelson, 2005. N. pag. Print.

7. Hancock, Jerry T. "Men in Balance Survey Results." *Survey Results*. Men in Balance, n.d. Web. 21 July 2017. <http://meninbalance.org/index.php/see-survey-results>.

8. Murrow, David. "Men: Who Needs 'Em?" *Why Men Hate Going to Church*. Nashville, TN: Thomas Nelson, 2005. N. pag. Print.

Lesson Eleven: Bonus Chapter on Communication

1. "Ubiquity: The 7% Rule." *ACM*. N.p., n.d. Web. 22 July 2017. <http://ubiquity.acm.org/article.cfm?id=2043156>.

2. Tippett, Krista. "Words." *Becoming Wise: An Inquiry into the Mystery and Art of Living*. Farmington Hills, Mich: Thorndike, a Part of Gale, Cengage Learning, 2016. N. pag. Print.

Other Lessons

1. Hancock, Jerry T. "Men in Balance Survey Results." *Survey Results*. Men in Balance, n.d. Web. 21 July 2017. <http://meninbalance.org/index.php/see-survey-results>.

2. Hancock, Jerry T. "Men in Balance Survey Results." *Survey Results*. Men in Balance, n.d. Web. 21 July 2017. <http://meninbalance.org/index.php/see-survey-results>.

Going Forward

1. *The Tale of Two Brains*. Dir. Mark Gungor. Perf. Mark Gungor. Laugh Your Way to a Better Marriage, n.d. Film.

Other Services of Men in Balance™

Small Group Discussion

We will help you establish a small discussion group in your church or other organization to discuss the more than 15 topics in the Men in Balance curriculum or this book specifically. Where possible, we will attend the kickoff session and provide training for your facilitator.

Men's Ministry Consulting for Churches

We will work with you to develop and execute a dynamic Men's Ministry or enhance your current efforts.

Individual or Couples Coaching

Affordable hourly rate for coaching individuals or couples on the topics in this book or other relationship issues, in person or via Skype or other electronic means.

Speaker for Retreats, Conferences

We will provide a reasonably priced dynamic presentation on men's issues for conferences, retreats or special meetings.

A free, no-obligation exploratory session is available for any of these services. For more information:

Men in Balance™
20908 N. Main Street
Cornelius, NC 28031
704.895.9676
www.meninbalance.org
jerry@meninbalance.org

www.ingramcontent.com/pod-product-compliance
Lightning Source LLC
LaVergne TN
LVHW010059170826
845678LV00012B/2182

* 9 7 8 0 6 9 2 9 2 8 3 1 8 *